Stop Calling Me Beautiful is a book every Christian woman needs to read. Phylicia breaks down "pink fluff" women's theology that has infiltrated the church and then builds a firm foundation on the true gospel that sets us free. If you're tired of surface-level teaching and shallow faith, this book will ignite a fire in your soul for a deeper walk with Jesus and draw you into the depths of the Word.

Gretchen Saffles, founder of Well-Watered Women

In a culture of so many vaporous words, *Stop Calling Me Beautiful* fed me on the substance of God's nature and His Words over my life. I closed the pages of this rich book and wanted more…of Him and His Word.

Sara Hagerty, bestselling author of *Unseen* and *Every Bitter Thing Is Sweet*

Stop Calling Me Beautiful is a strong, clear call for Christian women who long for a deeper, richer life and yet find themselves caught up in a feel-good, self-help, image-obsessed culture. Get ready to powerfully experience the thriving, transforming faith God intends for you.

Lisa Jacobson, author, cohost of the *Faithful Life* podcast, founder of Club31Women.com

Stop Calling Me Beautiful reveals how surface-level desires can keep us from soul-deep satisfaction. With honesty, clarity, kindness, and wisdom, Phylicia Masonheimer beckons us toward the greater depth—and true beauty—of biblical thinking, believing, and living.

Karen Swallow Prior, author of *On Reading Well* and *Fierce Convictions*

Our generation of women needs this book. *Stop Calling Me Beautiful* will not only take you deeper in your faith but will also motivate, challenge, and empower you to keep going deeper after the last page.

Valerie Metrejean Woerner, author of *Grumpy Mom Takes a Holiday*

STOP CALLING ME BEAUTIFUL

PHYLICIA MASONHEIMER

HARVEST HOUSE PUBLISHERS
EUGENE, OREGON

Cover design by Faceout Studio

Cover photo © Kkgas / Stocksy

Published in association with Books & Such Literary Management, 52 Mission Circle, Suite 122, PMB 170, Santa Rosa, CA 95409-5370, www.booksandsuch.com.

Stop Calling Me Beautiful
Copyright © 2020 by Phylicia Masonheimer
Published by Harvest House Publishers
Eugene, Oregon 97408
www.harvesthousepublishers.com

ISBN 978-0-7369-7800-2 (pbk)
ISBN 978-0-7369-7801-9 (eBook)

Library of Congress Cataloging-in-Publication Data

Names: Masonheimer, Phylicia, author.
Title: Stop calling me beautiful / Phylicia Masonheimer.
Description: Eugene : Harvest House Publishers, 2020.
Identifiers: LCCN 2019032718 (print) | LCCN 2019032719 (ebook) | ISBN 9780736978002 (trade paperback) | ISBN 9780736978019 (ebook)
Subjects: LCSH: Christian women--Religious life.
Classification: LCC BV4527 .M2688 2020 (print) | LCC BV4527 (ebook) | DDC 248.8/43--dc23
LC record available at https://lccn.loc.gov/2019032718
LC ebook record available at https://lccn.loc.gov/2019032719.

Printed in the United States of America

20 21 22 23 24 25 26 27 / BP-SK / 10 9 8 7 6 5 4 3

To all the women of strength, depth, and holy curiosity
who have gathered in my life and in my home:

You inspired this.
You anchored this.
You live this.

—

And to Adeline and Geneva:

May you become women
capable, confident, and complete in Christ.

CONTENTS

THE CHAPTER
BEFORE THE FIRST

attended my first Bible study when I was 16 years old. I came into
the house clutching my copy of Beth Moore's *Believing God* and
spent the next 16 weeknights glued to my pastor's TV screen. I still
remember the homework from that study and how I diligently filled
in the blanks and sat spellbound watching the videotaped lectures.

The study was my first taste of a deeper spiritual life. Though
raised in a Christian home, I had little interest in or desire for Christianity until I turned 15. By that point I'd been captive to a secret
struggle for three years (more to come about this in chapter 8). I was
desperate for a Christianity that was real. I wanted something that
made a *difference* in my life.

Like most Christian girls, I knew I should read my Bible, pray,
attend church, and have Christian friends, and I did all these things.
But something was missing. Jesus was a theory more than a person.
I read my Bible, but it was like I closed it on Him when I got up to

WHEN I BEGAN
SEARCHING FOR GOD
FOR GOD'S SAKE,
I DISCOVERED THE
KIND OF SPIRITUAL
WALK JESUS CAME
TO INITIATE.

go. I could defend Christianity intellectually, rationally, even emotionally, but God wasn't real to me *spiritually*. I floated on the surface of my faith and no one noticed, because most Christian women and girls were just like me.

Everything changed in college. I attended a Christian college in Virginia, and during my time there I met women who knew Jesus like Beth Moore did. They loved Him deeply. They served Him passionately. Their lives were so different from the cyclical patterns of defeat, guilt, and fear I knew. *How do I get that?* I wondered.

What I wanted was a life of victory. I wanted a spiritual life that was more than cute mugs emblazoned with the words "Beautiful Woman of God." I saw the promises Jesus made in Scripture and was puzzled by the disconnect. If Jesus promised overcoming, victorious, abundant life, why wasn't I experiencing it? Why was my own life riddled with anger, criticism, sexual struggles, and insecurity? How could women like Beth and my college friends talk about God as if He were right there, speaking to them through the Bible, while I opened it and only felt bored, the words dry?

I asked a lot of questions in this journey. I began digging into Scripture, reading my Bible not just to memorize Christian behaviors but to know God *Himself*. I figured if other women could know Jesus in a personal way, I could too. So I started with what I had: the Word of God.

As my eyes were opened to God's character in the Bible, my entire outlook was transformed. I saw that Christianity wasn't just about *me*—my faith, my study, my growth, my *self*—but was ultimately about God. It seems like such a basic conclusion, but it was profound in the moment.

Until then I'd been seeking Jesus to learn more about myself. I sought Him to find peace or to get away from the effects of my sin. I followed Him, but mainly as a means to an end, and my spiritual life reflected that. When I began searching for God for God's sake, I discovered the kind of spiritual walk Jesus came to initiate. I discovered what He meant by His promise that He had come to give us abundant life (John 10:10).

My journey to know God hasn't ended, and it never will. As my relationship with Him has grown and deepened, so has my desire for women to know the same spiritual depth I'm finding day by day. In today's culture, this is more vital than ever. There are thousands of women's ministries and women attempting to minister apart from a biblical foundation. The lines between true Christianity and self-help are blurred. Women come to Jesus by grace through faith, but then live as if Jesus has no power. They attend their churches, read devotionals, pray at dinner, and maybe even talk about their faith with their friends, but their inner lives are marked by emotional turmoil and daily defeat. They live with rigid rules or uncontrollable addictions, controlling spirits, and untamed tongues. Everything they were before Christ, just with fire insurance. I know what it looks like. I've been there.

But true spiritual depth and a life of eternal impact cannot happen apart from the Holy Spirit and God's Word, what we see transforming the first believers—people marked by their desire for God, hungry hearts, and love for one another (Acts 2:42-47). The Holy Spirit and the Word are still transformative today. But until we grasp how Jesus meets us in the difficult, hard, overwhelming parts of our lives, our faith will only be theoretical. We won't need the Word or the Spirit because we think we can self-help our way out of everything.

But can we?

I don't know about you, but the guilt, shame, and restlessness I experienced in my shallow faith (if you could even call it that) weren't what I wanted to experience during my time on earth. I thirsted for more. Most women do. We need more than "pink fluff" theology of out-of-context Bible verses, compliments to our personalities that never challenge us to grow, and topical messages about womanhood and identity. We are tired of the Bible being watered down and made palatable. We need and want *truth*, because only truth will set us free.

I can say with gratitude that God has freed me from the cycle of guilt and defeat I once knew as a shallow Christian. Overcoming, victorious, abundant life is here. It is *now*. It doesn't always look the way we expect and it's not easy to walk out, but it is available through Christ. He offers a relationship that changes everything.

PART ONE

1

STOP CALLING
ME BEAUTIFUL

re you ready to be encouraged, ladies?" The speaker sprang onto the stage with energy, her jewelry glittering in the stage lights. We shouted a collective "Yes!" from our seats as the speaker took her place at the pulpit. We'd already sung a few songs and played a game guessing what was inside someone's purse, and now were ready to be filled up with the Word. Trendily dressed in skinny jeans and big earrings, we grasped our journaling Bibles and monogrammed notebooks. We were excited and anxious to be encouraged, to find a solution to our daily struggle in this Christian life.

The speaker started with some relatable problems: Our need to feel like enough. Our stress. Our dissatisfaction with life as it is. "Ladies, we need Jesus!" she declared. "We need to be encouraged by Him so we can be the best wives and mothers and women we can be." We all got out our pens to take notes, ready to learn and grow. But as the message wore on between comedy segments, I heard nothing I hadn't heard before: "You're so beautiful." "You're so worthy of love. God will get you through this." "You just need Jesus."

The women nodded along with the message. I nodded along too. I knew I needed Jesus. The speaker was right about that. But as the evening ended and I shuffled out with the throng, Bible unopened under my arm, I wondered, *Is it normal to want more than this?*

Every year thousands of women gather together to listen to yet another speaker tell us who we are in Christ. These conferences, retreats, and conventions are well-intentioned. Some of them equip and educate women in the Word of God, or at least attempt to do so. Then the next year rolls around and we find ourselves once again seated at the women's conference, learning once again that we're "beautiful daughters of God." Yet each year we return home to the same struggles and sins we had before the conference. The spiritual high of the speaker's message fades. Something is missing.

At home, many of us face difficult marriages, lonely workplaces, unfriendly mirrors, and overwhelming motherhood. Insecurity and guilt take a backseat at a women's conference, but here at home? They loom large. The Jesus whose presence was so tangible in a worship-filled sanctuary is now seemingly impossible to reach.

The problem of shallow Christian teaching pervades women's conferences, retreats, ministries, and devotional books. We have heard the same message time and time again—a message meant to empower us to live better lives. Yet no matter how many times we hear it, change evades us. If this message is so powerful, why haven't our lives, marriages, and experiences of motherhood changed for the better? Why does the Christian life still feel so heavy if Jesus promised His burden was light (Matthew 11:30)?

The Christian life is not a checklist, but many women treat their faith as if that's exactly what it is. Their faith consists of virtues they are meant to achieve by sheer willpower and sufficient Bible reading.

They attend church, listen to worship music, start Bible-reading plans, and try to pray. But when anxiety, stress, fear, anger, or temptation assault their hearts, these women are running on empty. The Christian life they've been sold is all effort and little reward. The best they can hope for is the next platitude from their morning devotional—"You're a beautiful daughter of God!" However, the "you're beautiful" message, though palatable and fun to present, isn't the one women need to hear most.

Perhaps you're tired of the struggle. You're tired of the work. You're just…tired. And being told you're beautiful hasn't made things any easier. What good is being a beautiful daughter of the King when your marriage is on the rocks, when grief is choking you, when work is unfulfilling, or when you hate what you see in the mirror?

Women face many difficulties in our daily lives, things we never expected and never wanted. This is life in a fallen world, and Christianity is supposed to have an answer for our struggles. But the answers we've been given aren't helping us live more peaceful and victorious lives. We're still down in the mud and the broken places, wondering how this could possibly be what Jesus meant when He said, "My yoke is easy and my burden is light" (Matthew 11:30).

AN INCOMPLETE GOSPEL

Gospel is a vague word for many people, conjuring images of Billy Graham rallies and the hymnbook in Grandma's church. But the gospel is simply this: the whole story of Christ's work to save us.

What we hear from the pages of a devotional or the stage at a women's conference may feel right, but is it the stuff of freedom? We all want to know we're desirable, but will being called beautiful give us lives of purpose and depth? Judging by the results so far, the answer to both these questions is no. Being told we're beautiful in God's eyes is a surface response to a soul-deep problem. That problem is our own sinfulness.

Sinfulness isn't a word we like to attribute to ourselves. It's uncomfortable and ugly. We'd much rather talk about God's love for us—and that's what many female writers and teachers do. But when we ignore the impact of sin on our own natures, we can't comprehend the greatness of God's love. In John 3:16, Jesus says, "God so loved the world that he gave his one and only Son." God does love us—so much so that He sacrificed His Son. But when we focus only on the first half of this verse, we're missing the entire point. God doesn't love us because you and I deserved it. He loves us in spite of ourselves. We are so sinful, so unable to bridge the gap between ourselves and a holy God, that He sent His Son to die on our behalf.

As women, we long to know that we're desired just for being us. We'd much rather God had come to earth simply because we're beautiful to Him. But in order to grasp the fullness of God's love and find true freedom, we have to get the story straight. Sin marred our original beauty. Sin destroyed what God meant us to be.

God is life, and as sinners, we are separated from Him. This is why the apostle Paul said, "The wages of sin is death" (Romans 6:23); death is the ultimate separation from God. Apart from Jesus, that's just what will happen to us. Jesus's sacrifice wasn't just a nice plan to get us out of trouble. His punishment *replaced ours*! Because God *so loved* the world, Christ paid the debt we owed.

This is the gospel. This is the good news of Christ Jesus for those in need! But many female Christian leaders have parsed the gospel into "pleasant" and "not-so-pleasant" pieces. Consequently, we hear a lot about God loving us, calling us beautiful, and celebrating us as women, but not much about what had to happen for us to receive this extraordinary love.

BEING TOLD WE'RE
BEAUTIFUL IN GOD'S
EYES IS A SURFACE
RESPONSE TO A
SOUL-DEEP PROBLEM.
THAT PROBLEM IS OUR
OWN SINFULNESS.

The incomplete gospel of modern Christianity gives general solutions to very specific problems. Our struggle against sin manifests itself in specific ways: addiction, anger, fear, legalism, shame, and so much more. The problem for women today is the "good news" preached to women doesn't have the necessary depth to free us. It's not enough for Christian women, and we deserve more. We deserve to know the complete gospel and to understand how it frees us to live lives of both present and eternal impact.

The gospel is good news because it gives hope to the hopeless. It lifts us out of perpetual defeat and offers us a way home. A message divorced from the complete gospel, a message of love and beauty without Jesus's sacrifice, can never bring lasting change. The gospel is *the* specific solution to our specific problem with sin, however it manifests in our lives.

THE DEFEAT OF INCOMPLETENESS

What does the gospel have to do with our daily life? Everything. The defeat we experience in relationships and in temptation happens because we don't know how to rightly live out the gospel. And often we don't live out the gospel because we haven't heard it taught accurately. Many of us assume that if God loves us (a word we often define emotionally) and we love Him back on an emotional level, somehow we will live a life of eternal impact. This might satisfy us during an early-morning quiet time with coffee and a candle, but that kind of faith crumbles when we face conflict.

In crisis, we discover just how weak this gospel is. In the midst of a marital fight, a debilitating illness, or a sudden financial setback, knowing we are beautiful daughters of God falls rather flat. There has to be more to the gospel, the more that Jesus promised in John 10:10. And there is! The complete gospel—our sinfulness, God's grace, Christ's imputed beauty—empowers us with a strength the incomplete gospel cannot supply. Without the whole truth about who we are and what God does for us, we will never know the fullness of the life God intends for us.

So we need the full story, the whole gospel. The complete gospel enables us to live free from sin, shame, defeat, and stress. Yes, God loves us—but that love came with the highest of costs: Jesus's death on the cross. Acknowledging our own sinfulness is the first step to realizing the magnitude of God's love. When women recognize the lengths to which God went in order to bring them into His family, they are transformed. The bondage of besetting sins becomes surmountable. Chains of addiction are broken one by one. Challenges, fears, and difficulties that could not be conquered by an incomplete gospel are crushed by the power of complete truth.

Our God is a God of freedom. While we live in a fallen world, Christ has overcome the world (John 16:33). Every day that we walk by the Spirit of God, we have what we need to conquer weakness and sin. But it takes more than a feel-good message and an occasional prayer to get there.

WHERE THE MESSAGE WENT WRONG

The "beautiful daughter of God" message is not untrue. In Christ, we are indeed beautiful. We were also created in the image of God and are part of His kingdom work. These are beautiful truths. But the beauty of God's people is not the point of the gospel. The goal of the gospel is to unite us in relationship with our holy, loving God, and to invite others to have that relationship through our witness in this world.

Though it's comfortable and pleasing to hear positive and encouraging things about ourselves, that's not what women of God need

most. Shallow Christian messages try to affirm who we are in Christ
without discussing the consequences of sin. But sin is the problem.
We need the external solution to our internal sinfulness: We need
Jesus Christ. We need to hear less about us, and more about *Him*.

Hearing Jesus preached, not to learn more about ourselves or to
become better people, but simply to learn more about Him, is not
all that appealing to us. We want to know we're desirable, so messages about desirability strike a chord in our hearts. But if we want
to be truly free, we have to recognize the flaws in these narratives and
open ourselves up to something deeper, something far more lasting
than beauty and desirability.

There are three primary problems with the messages of many
female Christian influencers. By recognizing these three problems,
we can learn to see past surface-level gospel messages and seek the
truth that changes lives.

The Message Is Theologically Deficient

The first problem is that Christian women are being taught a
message that is theologically deficient. *Theology* has a simple defini-
tion: the study of God. Early church father Augustine defined it as
"an account or explanation of the divine nature."[1] All of us have a theology. Our theological viewpoint is the framework for our understanding of God. Everything you've read, heard, and believed about
Jesus and the Bible helped shape your understanding of who God is
and how He works in your life. This is your theological viewpoint.

Modern women's ministry's framework for presenting and
understanding God contains pieces of truth, but these pieces do
not present an accurate picture of God and the gospel. Women walk
away with a Christianity that is all verses and flowery feelings and
has no power for daily life.

We've been sold a message of all comfort and no strength, and because of this, many of us find following Christ joyless, hard, and empty. We can't conquer insecurity, shame, and feeling overwhelmed because all we know about God are proof-texted verses about His love and kindness. We don't know how to walk by the Spirit. We don't know the why and how of our salvation and how it works out in the hard hours of our days. These surface-level messages to women, though well-intentioned, are keeping us from a true knowledge of God and in bondage to the very things from which we want to be free.

The Message Is Self-Focused

Second, the message we're hearing is *self-focused*. Flawed theology always turns attention away from God and onto ourselves, and that's exactly what has happened with women's ministry today. The messages preached to us almost inevitably focus on…us. While it might seem logical that if we focus on ourselves more, we'll change ourselves for the better, that's not how discipleship works. Turning our eyes to Jesus is how we are transformed. Change comes by His power, not ours.

Self-focus is why so many Christian women are exhausted by the Christian life. Our attention is constantly being turned away from the One who could bring us real change. Instead, all our efforts are turned toward ourselves: our identities, our desirability, our inadequacy, and our work to be good Christian women. No wonder we're tired! This is not what God wanted for His daughters.

The Message Is Superficial

Finally, the modern messages preached to women through books and media lack *depth*. In an effort to provide relevant, relatable content to Christian women, we've watered down the gospel. The resulting content leaves women grasping for something more. Modern American expressions of Christianity, especially among women,

CUTE INSTAGRAM QUOTES, BIBLE VERSES, AND 15-MINUTE QUIET TIMES ARE NOT THE SUM OF THE CHRISTIAN LIFE.

are focused on the emotional, rather than intellectual, aspects of faith. With their limited knowledge of Scripture, Christian women are left ill-equipped to defend what they believe in the public sphere and are even less equipped to face testing.

Theological education—learning about God, the Bible, and how these truths apply to life—is not just for men or for those called to ministry. Women must be spiritually equipped with the knowledge of God through His Word so they can minister to the people around them. This requires participating in a depth of study to which many women aren't accustomed. Such education requires more spiritually mature women to disciple their weaker sisters. We must recognize that cute Instagram quotes, isolated Bible verses, and 15-minute quiet times are not the sum of the Christian life, but that we are called to a deep, consistent relationship with God and to teach that relationship to the people around us.

God's Word contains all we need to know about the Christian life, and we need to go deeper in our understanding of it. But we also need to know how to live it out. How many of us don't know what taking captive our thoughts (2 Corinthians 10:5) really means? How many of us don't know how to set our minds on the Spirit (Romans 8:6)? How many of us don't know how to walk in a manner worthy of our calling (Ephesians 4:1)? Ultimately, many of us don't know how our faith applies to marriage, motherhood, dating, or work. The missing piece of the conversation is the work of the Holy Spirit in the believer's life.

The Holy Spirit can make for a controversial topic. Large populations of Christians associate the Holy Spirit with charismatic churches, so many pastors and teachers avoid discussing the role of the third person of the Trinity. As a result, women do not know how the Spirit empowers them to overcome daily struggles.

Think for a moment. When was the last time you attended a

women's conference where the Holy Spirit was *really* talked about? What was the last book you read that taught you how the Spirit changes your relationships and helps you overcome sin? By avoiding controversy, conflict, and discussion of the Spirit's role, modern women's ministry remains on the surface of Christian teaching. This may be the safe way to teach, but it does not create thriving disciples. The beauty-centric gospel is responsible for creating a generation of female Christians who know little about what they believe or how those beliefs should play out on a daily basis.

THE MESSAGE WE NEED

A few weeks ago I attempted the Whole30 meal plan. I'd done it before—30 days without sugar, dairy, legumes, or processed food—but for some reason, this time was even more of a struggle. I made it for two weeks before we went out of town on a trip, during which I went completely off the plan. Donuts, here I come! Upon returning home, I found myself craving the foods that previously seemed so limiting. Having experienced the vibrancy of life without sugar, all I wanted was veggies and fruits.

Just as my body craved healthy food instead of sugary snacks, Christian women crave spiritual depth. They don't just *need* more from the church—they *want* more. Within every woman is both the ability and the desire to find a deeper spiritual life. Many women simply don't know where to start. We're told that Christ provides purpose, yet we live as if He doesn't. We're taught a Christianity based on effort, not gospel grace, and we are exhausted. We need a complete gospel message that includes who we are apart from God, reverence for God Himself, and how God enables us to overcome in daily life. But where to begin? Where do we find this message, and how do we live it out?

Within each woman of God dwells the Spirit of God, who grants us wisdom to comprehend who He is (John 14:26), but we don't know how to access that wisdom. We have the capacity to be curious about spiritual things. But surface-level messages kill such a curiosity. In a sense, many Christian influencers talk down to us instead of speaking to the capability of the Spirit within us. These messages are just enough to keep us going in our spiritual walk, but not enough to aid deeper growth.

The true gospel is available to all of us through God's Word. We must learn to study it. We must know it well enough to rightly divide the truth and check teachings against the Word of God as the Bereans did (Acts 17:11). In other words, we must cultivate a *holy curiosity*.

Holy means set apart, sacred, and dedicated to God. *Curiosity* is a strong desire to know and learn. A holy curiosity, then, refers to a mind that strongly desires to know and learn about God. A mind like this doesn't happen by accident. It is cultivated day by day. The Holy Spirit grows and nurtures this desire as we faithfully expose ourselves to Him through Scripture, godly community, and solid teaching (all of which we'll address later in this book).

Women who love God and cultivate this holy curiosity aren't satisfied with shallow teaching. By rejecting this imitation spirituality and seeking God's intentions for our walk with Him, we grow into a robust faith, a faith able to weather even the most difficult or mundane of circumstances: the death of a parent, the betrayal of a friend, the pain of infertility, the fear of financial ruin, the difficulty of long-term singleness.

Are you done living on the surface? Are you ready to dive deeper in your faith, your understanding of God, and your walk by the Spirit? Are you hungry for *more* and *better* in your spiritual life? If so, keep reading.

2

HUNGRY FOR MORE AND BETTER

Cassie started attending church in her late teens when one of her friends invited her to her youth group. Shortly after, she accepted Christ as her Savior. Thanks to diligent youth leaders, she knew the basics of the Christian faith, but she didn't understand how it all fit together in daily life. After she graduated from high school, she no longer had her youth leaders to answer her questions. She continued following the Lord, but did so in inconsistent spurts of Bible study, which often proved frustrating and dry.

In college, she joined a church Bible study for women, but even this taught her very little beyond what she already knew. She wanted to learn more, but she didn't have direction or consistent discipleship. The women leading her study didn't either, even though they were older than she was. She found herself struggling with the same sins over and over again, never getting victory. *Is this it?* she found herself asking. *Is this all it means to be a Christian?*

Fast-forward a few years and Cassie is married with kids. Bible study is harder now than ever before, as the demands of life fill her waking hours. She wants to be closer to her husband. She wants to stop yelling at her kids. She wants to know more about God and have godly community. But nothing she's ever learned about Christianity has penetrated that surface level. She feels ill-equipped to dive deeper. What if her conclusions are wrong? Isn't a pastor supposed to tell her what to think? How does any of it apply to life practically? Where does she start?

Cassie isn't alone in her struggle. There is a Cassie in all of us, a woman desiring to go deeper, to be challenged, to know God better. But unless we're in the right place at the right time with the right people, finding the resources to develop a deeper spiritual life is confusing and hard. We want so much to be women of faith, but God is a person we only know on paper. We are baffled when we hear others talk about their experiences in the presence of God. We marvel at the answers to their prayers. And we wonder, *Why doesn't that happen for me?*

We already know one answer to that question: Christian women have been receiving theologically watered-down messages for years. We need a change. But how?

Perhaps you've heard the phrase "The desire is half the battle." Isn't that true with any goal? If we want to lose weight, we have to first embrace the desire for change. Only then will we change our eating habits and start a workout schedule. The same goes for our walk with the Lord. Until we desire a deeper understanding of God, we'll settle for the half-hearted messages we've been given up to this point.

But desire for God is an elusive thing. Some days we long to know God with great fervor. Other days we fall asleep on our Bibles. If we base our pursuit of God only on our feelings, we'll never be consistent. Desire is a necessary part of deepening our relationship with the Lord, but it's not possible in our own strength. We need transformed desires and hearts reflective of His.

Psalm 37:4 says, "Delight in the LORD, and he will give you the desires of your heart." We might assume if we "delight" in God, He'll give us the things, jobs, and relationships we want. But when God promises us the desires of our hearts if we delight in Him, what He's promising is the blessing of a long-term, thriving relationship with Christ. As we pursue a deep, lasting relationship with our Savior, the desires of our hearts change. We stop satisfying ourselves with the cheap and easy—social media, alcohol, men—and learn to desire our Creator above all things. Desire and delight become an endless circle in the presence of the living God. This is the kind of deep relationship women crave, and it's the kind they've been distracted from by the "easy gospel": a gospel light on sin, heavy on personal satisfaction, and divorced from redemptive power.

GOING DEEPER

A deeper spiritual life doesn't happen by accident. Strong faith in Christ is a journey, a journey made up of days, hours, and minutes dedicated to knowing who God is.

Many Christian books promise to help us go deeper with the Lord. But the steps to get there often center on "finding oneself" in Christ. We learn all about womanhood, femininity, personality, and identity, with verses to back up this information. But authors use these verses in ways they were not intended: tearing biblical passages limb from limb, removing (or ignoring) historical and literary context, overlooking an author's intent. So when we finish reading we're left in the same place we began: dealing with our fallen selves, psyching ourselves into happiness with Bible verses about God's love. We think that if we can just discover who we are in Christ, we'll finally change. But the more we know ourselves, the more failure we see.

God-defined beauty and our purpose in God's kingdom are not to be ignored. Personality tests like the Enneagram and the Myers-Briggs Type Indicator can help us learn how to better communicate and address our weaknesses. But reading more about ourselves won't show us how to go deeper with God, because we're not focusing on the one who matters. We're still focusing on ourselves. Going deeper spiritually requires a shift of focus. We must turn our eyes away from our failures and successes, our ugliness and our God-given beauty, and instead fix our eyes on the perfection of Jesus Christ.

Our self-discovery is not God's goal. We are meant to know God and make Him known. This is the great adventure for which our hearts long! We are part of God's kingdom story. He didn't need us, but He chose to include us in His work. When we crave more in our walk with Him, that's the Spirit calling us to a place of security and rest. With God, we no longer endlessly seek affirmation and purpose. As the early church father Saint Augustine so poignantly stated, "Ours hearts are restless till they find their rest in thee."[1]

WHY WE DON'T EXPERIENCE GOD

Early on in my spiritual walk, I met a girl who seemed to have a line directly to the throne room. This girl was *on fire* for Jesus. Not only that, she prayed like God was right there with her, and the answers to her prayers were specific and clear. When she worshipped in church, she didn't care what anyone thought of her. She would kneel or raise her hands or go forward for prayer without hesitation. She seemed like a super-Christian. I admit, I was intimidated. But at the same time, I knew her relationship with God wasn't just a series of actions. She *loved* Jesus. She experienced Him in a real way. She had something I wanted, but I didn't know how to get it. I hungered for more, and knew if the hunger wasn't satisfied, I would no longer feel the hunger at all.

Have you ever been so hungry that you stop feeling hunger pangs? That's what happens when we consistently feed on shallow teaching. We stop hungering for richer spiritual teaching because our drive for it is gone. We're bored and uninterested in spiritual things because we're not being challenged to stretch our minds, hearts, and spirits. And because our hearts become uninterested in pursuing God on a deeper level, we never experience Him the way we could.

Hebrews 6:1 says, "Let us move beyond the elementary teachings about Christ and be taken forward to maturity." God's heart is for our spiritual growth, because it is through spiritual maturity that we know Him more intimately and become more effective for the kingdom of God. We cannot mature into deeper, stronger women if we remain in the shallow end of Christianity—as the author of Hebrews put it, the "elementary teachings" about Jesus Christ.

If you pray and don't see answers, if you read the Bible and end up yawning, or if you check out mentally whenever God is brought up, your spirit is not tuned in to what God has for you. Perhaps you are a Christian with the Spirit of God residing within you, but you do not listen for Him. You do not persevere in prayer, especially when it's difficult or inconvenient. You do not take an interest in spiritual discussion because it seems irrelevant to your daily life. Because you have not *experienced* God the way you see others experiencing Him, you take no interest in Him.

But here is the irony: When we take no interest in God, we do not experience His presence. We don't see Him work powerfully through prayer because we don't pray diligently. We don't receive direction and answers because we don't persevere in asking. And we don't experience the earth-shattering awareness of God's presence through His Word because we don't spend enough time there to do so! We cannot expect to experience relationship with someone whose company we never seek. God is a pursuer, but He will not force you to choose Him. If you want to have a deeper relationship with the Lord, He offers you every opportunity, but you must be the one to take it.

Hunger for depth and purpose is God's way of drawing us into relationship with Him. It's a godly desire, one we should embrace and possess. And this hunger leads us to experience God in the thousand small, daily ways He longs to reach us, not just in the mountain-top moments. If your heart deeply longs to know Him, God can provide a more powerful experience at your kitchen sink than at the height of the recommitment emotion in a Christian concert venue.

God wants us to experience Him. But experiencing God doesn't begin with emotion. It begins with desire, and it is accomplished by diligence.

DILIGENTLY SEEK HIM

God gives us desire for Him through His Holy Spirit's work in our inner being. In Romans 10:14-15, Paul pointed out this necessary work of the Holy Spirit in our lives and God's intentional seeking of those who need Him:

> How, then, can they call on the one they have not believed in? And how can they believe in the one of whom they have not heard? And how can they hear without someone preaching to them? And how can anyone preach unless they are sent?

GOD WANTS US TO
EXPERIENCE HIM. BUT
EXPERIENCING GOD
DOESN'T BEGIN WITH
EMOTION. IT BEGINS
WITH DESIRE, AND
IT IS ACCOMPLISHED
BY DILIGENCE.

The Holy Spirit draws us to God. It is His calling after our heart, His pursuit, which opens our eyes to our need of Him—a concept called "enabling grace." We choose how we respond to God's pursuit. After we surrender to Christ as Savior, our standing before God is guaranteed by the blood of Christ. The theological term for this is *justification*. We are no longer separated from or under the wrath of God. We stand before Him in the name of Jesus, and because of His sacrifice, we are perfectly pure.

Apart from Christ, we are not beautiful, pure, or acceptable because all humankind possesses a fallen nature. Though God originally created humans as perfect creatures, humankind's sinful choice makes our purity impossible without Jesus. Just because we are justified by Jesus does not mean we will remain pure all our days on this earth. We still must make the daily choice to *live up* to our identity in Christ.

Our former self and the natural bent to our fleshly desires prevent us from reaching perfection this side of heaven. But each day we draw closer to Christ, deepening our understanding of and our relationship with Him, we become more and more like Him. This process is called *sanctification*. This theme recurs throughout Scripture, using terms such as *consecrated*, *set apart*, and *holy*. While justification is a one-time event at salvation (a change of status before God), sanctification is progressive. The process of being sanctified lasts all our lives and reaches fruition when we enter into glory (1 Thessalonians 5:23). And in order to become like Jesus, we must diligently seek Jesus. That's how sanctification works.

Though our seeking of Jesus starts with a desire to know Him more, those desires—like any emotion—come and go. You might be familiar with that resistance when, at six in the morning, the last thing you want to do is spend time in the Word. There are seasons when our desire for God is not as strong as it was before, perhaps due to stress, busyness, or personal circumstances. But that's where diligence comes into play. Those who push past their emotions with the conviction that God is still listening are those who diligently seek the face of Jesus. And those who diligently seek Him are rewarded: "Without faith it is impossible to please God, because anyone who comes to him must believe that he exists and that he rewards those who earnestly seek Him" (Hebrews 11:6). This is a beautiful promise. It lifts the weight of self-transformation and guarantees that we will be received by God when we seek Him first.

We don't go deeper with God by reflecting more on ourselves, or even by reading God's Word to look for insight about ourselves. Roots of spiritual growth develop as we seek God for who He is and allow Him to do the transforming work in our hearts that we can never do on our own. He is the one who plants the desire to seek Him. He is the one who meets us when we apply diligence in faith.

BUT WHERE DO WE START?

We know that God does the work in our hearts and lives—our justification and sanctification. But we also have to align ourselves with His will by doing the work of exposing ourselves to Him through His Word. This is where many women get overwhelmed. Most of us don't have religion degrees and will never attend seminary. How do we study the Bible and know God through its pages?

Jen Wilkin is my constant reference point when teaching women how to get started with Bible study. In her book *Women of the Word*, Jen teaches not only the practical how-tos of studying the Bible, but she also articulates how we should approach the Word. The state of our hearts and minds has a great influence on what we draw from the Bible. How we think about God guides our comprehension and application of each passage we read.

Resources like Jen's are a great start for learning how to "correctly [handle] the word of truth" (2 Timothy 2:15). But once you've learned the basics, Bible study is as simple as actually reading the Bible. You don't need to know everything up front to learn and appreciate what God says in His Word. But you *do* have to be willing to start. From that heart of willingness, you can add resources for deeper study. These will add depth to the places, people, and terms you read in the Bible, transforming what used to be drab and gray into the living color of God's redemption story.

You might be thinking, *This sounds so simple, but I've tried to study the Bible. My life keeps getting in the way.* Exposing ourselves to God's Word is not easy. The Enemy resists us in every way he can because he knows the power of a gospel-rooted believer. We must recognize this resistance and prepare ourselves for the distractions guaranteed to come our way.

When I was in high school, I usually spent time with God in the morning. I had a walk-in closet where I set up a corkboard, a CD player for worship music (it was a long time ago!), and a basketful of Bible study materials. I could easily spend 30 minutes to an hour studying the Word in that little room.

Fast-forward to college and my full-time career, and time with God was harder to come by. In this stage of my life, I often squeezed devotions into my lunch break or at 5:00 a.m. before work. Sometimes I'd walk to the campus prayer chapel, the only place that was quiet enough on my busy days. My quiet times were not as consistent as they had been in high school, and they certainly weren't at the same time each day. I often compared my new season to the old one, wondering if I was doing something wrong in my relationship with God if I couldn't meet Him in the way I used to.

Those seasons are now past, and I'm in a new one: as a work-at-home mom with two girls under the age of three. I've learned that going deeper with God isn't about where you meet Him or when; it's about showing up. As I write this, it's 4:30 a.m. I got up to nurse my four-month-old baby. Rather than go back to bed on these early mornings, I've been staying up to spend time with the Lord in the quiet. This is my season. I can resist it and miss out on God's presence, or I can embrace it and let Him call me deeper.

By letting go of the idea that there is an ideal quiet time, we allow ourselves the freedom to know God through His Word in the toughest of seasons. There is a historical beauty to this, for the gospel was recorded in seasons of difficulty much like the ones we face. The lives of Jesus, Peter, Paul, and those in the early church were constantly under attack through persecution, trial, and exhaustion. I am sure they didn't get a quiet time with coffee and an armchair! But they consistently sought God, and God showed up.

We have to get beyond the belief that we must have a perfect quiet time and the right devotional books and the dependence on others' interpretations to open God's Word for ourselves. We need the full gospel—the gospel that began in Genesis and runs to Revelation like a "scarlet thread," a continual story written in blood—in order to find a deeper spiritual life in this shallow world. Finding this life is not easy. It takes diligence. But diligence is what a student of any kind must cultivate in order to gain knowledge. And that's what we, as believers, need to do.

SEEK IN COMMUNITY

There is another aspect of deepening our walk with the Lord that the Western church (which is most of us) fails to prioritize: community. We consider our faith an individual affair, something between us and God. And in one sense that's true. But a personal relationship with God isn't the end of the story.

Christianity is a communal faith. Israel worshipped God corporately as His chosen nation, a light to the people around them. Each individual's obedience affected Israel as a whole. When Jesus came as the fulfillment of God's promise to Israel to send His Messiah to save people from their sins, the church became a community of Jews and non-Jews (Gentiles) grafted together into the redemptive hope of Jesus (Romans 11:11-31). This community of faith was, and still is, a group of individuals pointing to the goodness of God.

Unfortunately, Western Christians don't always understand or appreciate the communal nature of our faith. We are raised to emphasize individuality; we're told that blending in is a bad thing. We don't like to be affected by the actions of others. Individualism is hard for us to overcome, even when we desperately need other believers around us. Consequently, we don't put ourselves in community because we don't want to be vulnerable. We like to keep our business to ourselves, and we don't want others watching us struggle in the Christian life.

But despite what our Western minds prefer, God insists on our involvement in Christian community. We are called to vulnerability, transparency, and the sharing of our burdens. Without this, we cannot grow as believers.

At the beginning of this chapter, we talked about Cassie, a hypothetical Christian woman who found the Christian life underwhelming and dry. Cassie's church is what many Americans experience on a weekly basis: a place to come to sit and listen, then leave. Discipleship isn't expected of Cassie, and fellow believers aren't intentionally leading her deeper in her walk with God. In Cassie's church (and probably some of ours), discipleship is a ministerial responsibility, something only pastors are expected to do, not your average church member.

This model is not what God intended, and it's not what we see in the early church:

- "They devoted themselves to the apostles' teaching and to fellowship, to the breaking of bread and to prayer" (Acts 2:42).

- "Every day they continued to meet together in the temple courts. They broke bread in their homes and ate together with glad and sincere hearts" (Acts 2:46).

- "Day after day, in the temple courts and from house to house, they never stopped teaching and proclaiming the good news that Jesus is the Messiah" (Acts 5:42).

- "On the first day of the week we came together to break bread. Paul spoke to the people and, because he intended to leave the next day, kept on talking until midnight" (Acts 20:7).

Elsewhere in the New Testament we see further instructions to gather together, encouraging one another in our faith. We're told to bear one another's burdens (Galatians 6:1-3), to not forsake the gathering of believers (Hebrews 10:25), and to exhort one another daily (Hebrews 3:13). It is by seeking God *within community* that our faith-roots intertwine with others', forming a fruitful community that supports one another as it grows.

ABUNDANT LIFE BEGINS NOW

The more and better we want out of our Christian lives starts by desiring to know God. We grow as we recognize, embrace, and cultivate this desire by seeking God in His Word—even when we don't feel like it. We bear fruit as we plant ourselves in godly community.

God intends for us to know Him more and better, for us to constantly deepen our walk with Him. But we can't do that if we stay on the surface, and we can't do it alone. We can't draw near if we don't open our Bibles and read them ourselves, if we don't put ourselves into godly community, and if we don't receive discipleship and accountability. We live abundantly when we regularly expose ourselves to the work and Spirit of God. When we do, the things that used to bore us take on the color of abundant life.

WHAT YOU CAN DO TODAY

1. Think of a Christian message you have heard that was meant to encourage but ended up frustrating you. What about that message was incomplete? Did it concentrate on who God is or on who you are?

2. Let go of the idea of an ideal quiet time. How can you simplify drawing near to God through His Word? What will you do today to seek Him there?

3. Assess your community. Are you plugged into a church body? Are you cultivating relationships there or are you just showing up? Make a plan for (a) finding a church family if you don't have one and (b) connecting regularly with your church family if you do.

3

A TALE OF
TWO WOMEN

John 4 opens with Jesus journeying through the land of Samaria, a region between Judea and Galilee. As Jesus traveled northward, He purposely went through Samaria. He stopped at a well near the town of Sychar, and while waiting for His disciples, He met a woman who was not happy.

We know several facts about her:

- She was a Samaritan. Samaritans were despised by the Jews because they were descendants of Jews who had intermarried with Assyrian people. The Samaritans had as positive a view of the Jews as the Jews had of them.

- She had had five husbands and was now living with a sixth man.

- She was shocked to meet Jesus and be recognized by Him. The fact that Jesus (1) spoke to a woman, (2) spoke to a *Samaritan* woman, and (3) asked her for a drink were each countercultural in their own right. Together, they were absolutely astonishing.

The stage set in the first few verses of John 4 would have shocked the socks, or the sandals, off a Jewish reader in that day. Our Western minds don't recognize the impact at first. But as we journey through the story, we discover some incredible truths, not just about Jesus's interaction with the Samaritan woman, but about His heart for *all* women and their relationship with Him.

LIVING WATER
(John 4:6-15)

It was the sixth hour, most likely the sweltering heat of noon, and Jesus was tired. He sat on the edge of the well alone; His disciples had gone into the city to buy food. As the dust on the path settled down after His followers left, He saw a woman approaching.

The ensuing discourse moves quickly. Jesus opened by asking for a favor:

> When a Samaritan woman came to draw water, Jesus said to her, "Will you give me a drink?" (His disciples had gone into the town to buy food.) The Samaritan woman said to him, "You are a Jew and I am a Samaritan woman. How can you ask me for a drink?" (For Jews do not associate with Samaritans.) (verses 7-9).

Jesus not only acknowledged the Samaritan woman; He humanized her by requesting a favor from her hand. For a Jewish man, particularly a teacher, to do such a thing was remarkable—and it caught her interest. Jesus seized this opportunity, took the water, and began to discuss water of a different kind: "Jesus answered her, 'If you knew the gift of God and who it is that asks you for a drink, you would have asked him and he would have given you living water'" (verse 10).

"Living water." What did He mean? What did it mean for water to be alive? In earthly terms, living water is active water—water that continually rejuvenates itself, bubbling up, being restored and refreshed, never growing stale or stagnant. Jesus was making a visible analogy—an object lesson—between the woman's need for physical water and her desperate spiritual need. Like many of us, she had lived so long in parched, dehydrated spirituality that she barely recognized what had happened within her. Jesus took this moment to reawaken her. He used something she needs every day to reveal the emptiness of her soul. But she was skeptical:

> "Sir," the woman said, "you have nothing to draw with
> and the well is deep. Where can you get this living water?
> Are you greater than our father Jacob, who gave us the
> well and drank from it himself, as did also his sons and
> his livestock?" (verses 11-12).

Time for a history lesson. The well where Jesus and the Samaritan woman conversed was indeed Jacob's well, and Samaritans also traced their ancestry back to Jacob. It was their one claim to fame in a culture that constantly denigrated their ethnicity. You can almost feel the defensiveness rising off the page as we read the woman's words. We might paraphrase them this way: "Hey, mister, remember—we're related! We share a father, and *he* gave us this well. If it was good enough for Jacob, it should be good enough for you. You Jews think you are so much better. Who do you think you are?"

Jesus didn't get into a parley or engage her defensive retort. Instead, He directed the conversation back to her deepest need, a *spiritual* need, one that went beyond her ethnicity, identity, and family:

Jesus answered, "Everyone who drinks this water will be thirsty again, but whoever drinks the water I give them will never thirst. Indeed, the water I give them will become in them a spring of water welling up to eternal life." The woman said to him, "Sir, give me this water so that I won't get thirsty and have to keep coming here to draw water" (verses 13-15).

Jesus's offer was intriguing. The woman was excited at the thought of an easier life; who wouldn't be? She would never have to come to the well again. Her interest, now piqued, opened the door for the conversation Jesus wanted to have: a discussion of her brokenness.

BROKEN, BITTER, AND BEATEN DOWN
(John 4:16-19)

No one wants a complete stranger to know her innermost secrets. I don't know a woman alive who'd share her relationship history with a man she just met—particularly an authority figure and teacher like Jesus. We like to keep our skeletons where they belong: in the closet.

I picture Jesus, seated on the edge of the well as the woman draws the bucket, telling her about this living water. I see her hand Him a drink of it, her eyes wary and reserved, wondering why this man is talking to her and what this water He offers could be.

But at the peak of her interest, just when trust was being built, Jesus invaded the most painful part of the woman's life: "He told her, 'Go, call your husband and come back.' 'I have no husband,' she replied" (verses 16-17).

I have no husband. A simple statement, but one full of emotion. It revealed a little and hid so much. Jesus had lifted the lid on a story she wanted kept closed: *her* story, *her* brokenness, *her* shame. But in the same way Jesus went intentionally into Samaria, He intentionally pressed into the Samaritan woman's heart. "You are right when you say you have no husband. The fact is you have had five husbands, and the man you now have is not your husband. What you have just said is quite true" (verses 17-18).

Some commentators have said that this woman was a homewrecker, bouncing from husband to husband as she divorced the ones she didn't prefer. But given Judaic and Samaritan marital law in that day, this is impossible. Women did not have the right to divorce. What is more likely is that the Samaritan woman had been divorced, widowed, or some combination of the two. Though it is possible she committed adultery, men in that day could divorce a woman for the smallest offense, and it is probable (due to the number of divorces) that she was infertile and unable to bear an heir. Five times she married; five times she was unwanted or left behind. Five times she was left to live on her one security—her dowry, her only protection as a woman in a patriarchal culture. Five times neglected was five times too many, and in the end, she may have given up.

The Enemy has the same batch of lies he reuses in each successive age. Here he employed the lie of hopelessness: *You're too far gone for anything better.* Abuse of dignity often leads us to *give up* our dignity. The Samaritan woman needed a place to live, but maybe she was reluctant to marry again and hand off her dowry to yet another man. Maybe she was afraid to experience neglect and abandonment. Apart from God, there is little hope in a situation like this. So perhaps she kept her dowry. Perhaps she didn't marry again. Perhaps she traded her body for a roof over her head and sacrificed her dignity for security.

How familiar this sounds to many of us. We feel trapped by the pain of our past, unable to grasp the abundant life Jesus promises.

So we put on a tough façade and go about our daily tasks, meanwhile harboring a broken and beaten heart.

But in one sentence Jesus dismantled the Samaritan woman's tough façade. Everything she'd been hiding—the brokenness, the hurt, the neglect, and the shame—was pulled to the forefront by the man at the well. And He does the same for us. He invades the hardest places of our hearts to teach us the truth about abundant life.

If we were offering the kind of message typical of women's ministry, we'd stop there. Broken women meet Jesus, He shows them His love and kindness, and they leave feeling loved by Jesus in the middle of their mess—but just as broken as before. But this is not how the Samaritan woman's story ends. Her brokenness meets the love of Jesus, but there is something more to be done.

AN INCOMPLETE WORSHIP
(John 4:19-26)

By exposing the Samaritan woman's painful past, Jesus laid before her a choice: She could continue to hide what He already knew, or she could bring it into the open and see what this man at the well would do with her story.

The woman decided to stay, but she was defensive. "'Sir,' the woman said, 'I can see that you are a prophet. Our ancestors worshiped on this mountain, but you Jews claim that the place where we must worship is in Jerusalem'" (verses 19-20). Like most of us, she reacted to the exposure of her sin and shame by declaring a difference of belief systems. If she lived today, the Samaritan woman might say, "Look, you Jews have a different view of religion than I do. We do things differently here. Don't come here to tell me how to live my life." The Samaritans did not worship like the Jews. They had their own temple, followed only the first five books of the

Torah (Genesis–Deuteronomy), and even had their own separate location of worship: Mount Gerizim. This was a point of contention between Samaritans and Jews. It's interesting that the Samaritan woman pointed this out to Jesus right after *He* pointed out her brokenness and sin.

Over and over, we see Jesus's intentionality in this interaction. By pulling her past to the surface, He was not being arbitrary and cruel; He was simply showing her what she worshipped. He was opening her eyes to what she was trying hardest to protect: her identity, formed as it was by her culture and circumstances. He was pointing out her biased understanding of God's character. The Samaritan woman had an incomplete view of God, and thus an incomplete *worship* of God. Just as the incomplete gospel creates a flawed theology today, this incomplete worship caused the woman to live in perpetual bondage. Her broken past defined her. Abundant life evaded her.

Jesus's next words were like the sounds of shackles breaking:

> "Woman," Jesus replied, "believe me, a time is coming when you will worship the Father neither on this mountain nor in Jerusalem. You Samaritans worship what you do not know; we worship what we do know, for salvation is from the Jews. Yet a time is coming and has now come when the true worshipers will worship the Father in the Spirit and in truth, for they are the kind of worshipers the Father seeks. God is spirit, and his worshipers must worship in the Spirit and in truth" (verses 21-24).

Jesus told her, "You Samaritans worship what you do not know." The Greek word for "know" can also be translated "understand" or "pay attention to." The woman at the well worshipped what she did not understand. Her faith was shallow and based on incomplete information. Based on her conversation with Jesus, we can infer that she was going through *motions* of worship—attending the temple, performing the necessary rites—but she was not in active relationship with God. She did not *understand* what worship really was—grateful reverence directed to a personal and loving God. Sound familiar?

Brokenness becomes our identity when we live out a surface-level faith. Abundant life evades us because we don't understand what Jesus offers through the gospel. The Samaritan woman represents *every* person who is going through the motions of faith but failing to live out its overcoming power.

THE OTHER WOMAN AT THE WELL
(Genesis 34)

Let's put a bookmark in John 4 for a moment. There is a precursor to the woman at the well, a woman whose life was equally scarred by brokenness and shame. But her story ended much differently than the Samaritan woman's. To find her, we must turn to Genesis 34.

The narrative opened with Jacob, son of Isaac, son of Abraham, camping outside a city called Shechem. If you recall, Jacob was the mutual ancestor of both Jews and Samaritans. Jacob had 12 sons and probably several daughters, but only one daughter is named in Scripture: Dinah.

While camping at Shechem, Dinah decided to visit the "women of the land" (verse 1). While visiting, the prince of the city (and the city's namesake) raped her and then decided he wanted to marry her (verses 2-3). Dinah remained captive in Shechem's house while he, with his father, pursued Jacob's approval of the marriage.

Jacob should have been outraged. In ancient Middle Eastern

culture (and even today), to forcefully take a man's daughter was a shame on the aggrieved man's entire household. But Jacob did nothing (verse 5). He remained silent until his sons returned from tending the livestock.

Jacob's lack of outrage over Dinah's abuse was made up for by her brothers' response. Simeon and Levi were irate at the shame brought upon their sister and the household. They decided to trick Shechem, offering Dinah in marriage *if* all the men in the city would be circumcised, since to do otherwise would be "a disgrace to us" (verse 14). Three days later, "while all of them were still in pain, two of Jacob's sons, Simeon and Levi, Dinah's brothers, took their swords and attacked the unsuspecting city, killing every male" (verse 25). The slaughter of Shechem's men was meant to bring justice for Dinah and Jacob, but the effort was ill-received by Jacob:

> Then Jacob said to Simeon and Levi, "You have brought trouble on me by making me obnoxious to the Canaanites and Perizzites, the people living in this land. We are few in number, and if they join forces against me and attack me, I and my household will be destroyed." But they replied, "Should he have treated our sister like a prostitute?" (verse 30-31).

The account ends there, leaving us astonished by Jacob's selfishness, mortified by Simeon and Levi's violence, and heartbroken over Dinah's story. Like the Samaritan woman, Dinah had been neglected, abused, and deprived of her dignity. Her whole life was marred by this episode. The very thing meant to bring her justice would be her identifier: a long-standing story of her shame.

You might be wondering what Dinah's story has to do with the woman in John 4. Dinah's rape, and the ensuing shame of Jacob, happened in the *very place* where Jesus met the woman at the well.

The well outside Sychar in Samaria is the *same well* Jacob built by Shechem (Genesis 33:19). On this same ground walked two women, thousands of years apart. Both of them were broken, hurting, and burdened by shame. These two women have strikingly similar stories, but their stories end in drastically different ways.

FREE FROM SHAME
(John 4:27-30,39-41)

The shame of Dinah and the Samaritan woman seemed insurmountable in the patriarchal culture of their day. Even today, shame is overwhelming. It keeps us from drawing near to God. It drives us into a spiral of defeat. And it is perpetuated by misunderstanding the gospel Jesus offers.

The Samaritan woman's story could have ended just like Dinah's, but it didn't. After Jesus called her to true worship—the "more and better" He promises—she responded:

> "I know that Messiah" (called Christ) "is coming. When
> he comes, he will explain everything to us" (verse 25).

I picture Jesus's eyes looking gently into hers, piercing the deepest recesses of her heart. She knew *about* her Savior, but she didn't know Him personally. She knew *about* the hope awaiting her, but she did not know how close He really was. As she busied herself with her bucket, Jesus looked into that burdened, broken heart and told her, "I, the one speaking to you—I am he" (verse 26).

Here, in the midst of brokenness and defeat, the Samaritan woman met her Messiah. She was so thrilled by Him that "leaving her water jar, the woman went back to the town and said to the people, 'Come, see a man who told me everything I ever did. Could this be the Messiah?'" (verses 28-29). For the first time she could face her story without shame. She was so free from it, and she had no problem declaring that Jesus had exposed *everything* about her.

Jesus entered into her story with intention. He lovingly showed her the truth about her past and her worship. And He called her, not simply to know *about* Him, but to put down her water jar and look Him full in the face.

So many of us have stories that end like Dinah's: in silence and shame. We could lift our faces to the Savior, who is oh-so-near, but we try to fill ourselves up with temporary "water": relationships, social media, food, shopping, or careers. Our water jars are full and our hands are busy, but our hearts are empty and overcome by defeat.

This is not God's intention. God's intention is for you to live as an *overcomer*, whose story calls others to know their Messiah. Many Samaritans from that town believed in Him because of the woman's testimony: "We know that this man really is the Savior of the world" (verses 39-42).

Dinah saw an entire city destroyed because of her shame; the Samaritan saw an entire city saved because her shame was defeated. This is what happens when we no longer accept brokenness and half-hearted worship as a lifestyle. *This* is abundant life.

YOUR BROKENNESS
IS NOT YOUR IDENTITY

Your brokenness is real, but it is not your identity. It is not an excuse, and it is not your future. Your Savior is sitting beside you, whispering, "I am your Messiah." You can take hold of abundant, overcoming life—if you set down the water jar, turn to Jesus, and let Him show you a new chapter in your story. No matter what part of your life is broken, Jesus has overcome it. Now let's learn how to walk that out.

WHAT YOU CAN DO TODAY

1. Ask yourself, "What would life be like if I actually *lived* as an overcomer? If abundant life were a reality?"

2. Read through John 4 today as your Bible study passage. Write down anything you notice about how Jesus spoke to the Samaritan woman.

3. Have you acknowledged Jesus's desire to be the foundation and center of your life? Do you trust Him as your Messiah, not just eternally, but today?

4

WHY THE INSTAGRAM BIBLE WON'T FREE YOU

My alarm went off at 6:00 a.m., beeping obnoxiously in the dark. I rolled out of bed and rubbed my eyes. The day's activities of senior-year schoolwork and my part-time retail job awaited me, but that's not where my day began. It began in my closet.

My walk-in closet was part game room and part clothes storage, and it contained a large, bare wall that I'd transformed into my quiet time space. It was the Taj Mahal of Bible-study corners: A large corkboard took up most of the wall, covered in pictures of friends, prayer requests, quotes to remember, and Bible-study tips. A basket with my Bible, notebook, pens, concordances, and commentaries sat on the floor, and I even had a CD player with my favorite worship music. It was the place I loved to be the most when I was 17.

To this day, my five younger siblings still tease me about my "shrine." In my effort to do the Christian quiet time thing, I may have overdone it a little. As time passed, I switched rooms, left my parents' house, and then got married and had kids, and my quiet time hasn't looked the same since.

Modern evangelical Christianity, particularly among women, is propelled by the principle of quiet time. Even the term *quiet time* has become a Christian culture byword, the embodiment of devotion to God. "All I need is a little coffee and a whole lot of Jesus" might be written on shirts, but it's also written into our minds. And if we don't meet with God in the way we think we're supposed to, we struggle with a burden of guilt.

If there's one thing about female Christian culture that breaks my heart, it's how *great* we are at taking a pretty Instagram photo of our quiet time spot or tricking out our Bibles with trendy tabs and paint…and how *poor* we are at truly studying God's Word. As I write this, #biblejournaling has over 550,000 posts on Instagram. If you scroll through the images, you'll see beautiful hand lettering and phenomenal artwork etched into the pages of Psalms and Ephesians—sometimes to the point you can't read the text. There's nothing inherently wrong with beautifying a Bible. There's nothing wrong with celebrating God's Word through art. But there *is* something wrong when time with God acquires so many trappings that we miss the actual point of it.

The guilt we struggle with when we miss a quiet time might not be so heavy if we didn't add so much to something that should be so simple. The saints of the Old and New Testaments, as well as our sisters and brothers throughout the ages, rarely had the privilege of meeting with God in comfort. While we worry over whether 30 minutes is enough time as we prep our coffee mugs and gather our highlighters, the early church came to God and His Word as an exercise of faith. It didn't look perfect (Susanna Wesley threw her apron over her head to pray so her ten children knew she was spending

THE GUILT WE
STRUGGLE WITH
WHEN WE MISS A
QUIET TIME MIGHT
NOT BE SO HEAVY IF
WE DIDN'T ADD SO
MUCH TO SOMETHING
THAT SHOULD BE
SO SIMPLE.

time with God), but it was a cultivated habit (George Müller spent time in prayer immediately after getting dressed or took his Bible with him for a walk outside).

Their devotion to God was just that—*devotion*. The time spent with Him was something they lived out in the minutes and hours of the coming day; it was not just a stopping point before breakfast. The lives of our Christian forefathers reflected an inner devotion and communion with God that we cannot get from a surface-level time with Him. Their devotion to pursuing God through prayer and His Word—not just for self-improvement, but to engage in spiritual war—led them to live lives of incredible power. And all the high-lighters and sticky tabs in the world won't do that.

When I first studied the quiet time phenomenon, I mentioned it on Instagram. Someone messaged me, saying, "I've always wondered where the quiet time came from and if it's in the Bible. Obviously we see people rising early all over Scripture." But is getting up early to pray—the model put forth by Daniel, David, Jesus, and others—the same as our armchair-and-coffee stereotype?

THE ORIGINS OF THE QUIET TIME

Today's Christians talk about their quiet time as a *should*: "I know I *should* be meeting with God, praying, and reading my Bible. It's just so hard to be consistent." And it's true; consistency is tough. But what if the problem isn't consistency, but the quiet time concept itself? Did you know the words *quiet time* aren't found anywhere in Scripture? Understanding where they came from might shed light on where Christian culture is today in regard to personal devotion to Christ.

The term *quiet time* was first popularized in a pamphlet published by the Intervarsity Christian Fellowship.[1] It was quickly adopted by Campus Crusade for Christ, the Navigators, and Billy Graham. What used to be called "the morning watch"—a time focused on reading the Word and intercessory prayer (prayer on behalf of yourself, others, the church, and nations)—changed in focus from praying *to* God to listening *for* God.

One of the characteristic elements of evangelical devotion prior to 1920 was a strong emphasis on prayer. The Word was the basis for it, time was spent on it, and lives were changed through it. The earliest evangelical church fathers and writers, such as John Wesley, George Whitefield, and later Charles Spurgeon and Oswald Chambers, regularly espoused the necessity of prayer for a thriving Christian life, which included both appealing to and listening for God. The term *morning watch* reflected the military mind-set of many Western Christians of that time. They recognized life as a spiritual war, and their time with God was part of the battle.

But with the change of terminology in the 1940s came a slow change of devotional dynamic. As evangelical culture emphasized listening *for* God, devotional time with Him became less about prayer and obedience and more focused on passive spiritual disciplines—things like silence, stillness, and meditation.

Before, time with God was outward focused; prayer and time in the Word were meant to drive the believer to action. During the shift of focus from corporate action to individual pursuit, time with God became primarily inward focused. Cultural Christianity emphasized the individual as opposed to the believer's effect on her community. While quieter spiritual disciplines and listening to God's will for our individual lives are vital to our pursuit of Him, they become lopsided when they become disconnected from their purpose: building a faith that leads people to take action in the world.

This brings us to today. The resulting quiet time culture continues to emphasize listening for God, meditating on the Word, and being quiet and still. It also suffers from a severe case of self-focus. We come to God because of our relationship with Him, but we've forgotten that this relationship is meant to be a driving force for evangelism. Thus, what we learn in our Instagrammable quiet times makes us feel good but doesn't create Christ-followers who know what following Christ looks like or how to spread the message of the gospel to others.

Time with God in the twenty-first century is primarily focused on learning what God wants for *us.* We read the Word to learn how to apply it…to us. We pray to ask God more about ourselves. We listen to hear God's message for us. The morning watch is no longer a part of a bigger story. Devotional time has become more focused on personal fulfillment and less on eternal significance.

God is a personal God, and I'm in no way saying we should stop cultivating a deep relationship with Him through the spiritual disciplines. I firmly believe there is an important place for fasting, silence, solitude, and meditation in the Christian life. But there is also a necessary place for perseverant prayer and Spirit-motivated evangelism. When we become spiritually imbalanced, we end up spiritually ineffective. Our time spent with God should be focused on learning more about Him, and in doing so, we will learn how to view ourselves. It should also reflect the priorities we see modeled in the lives of God's followers in the Old and New Testaments. The apostle Paul probably never had a quiet time in the way we do, but his outward obedience reflected his inner devotion. Like Paul and the saints before us, we need to live lives of both strength and significance.

COMING BACK TO WORSHIP

As we've seen, drawing near to God has changed in emphasis over the years. While modern devotionals do tend toward self-focus, we can still cultivate thriving spiritual lives with the quiet time model. To do so, we must look beyond our modern practice to how our Christian predecessors approached God.

David's life with God is perhaps one of the most visible in the Bible, as many of his prayers are turned into psalms. He sought God in the morning (5:3) and on his bed (63:6). He praised God privately (Psalm 103:1) and publicly (27:4). He delighted in God's law (Psalm 25:4-5), which is the Old Testament to us today, and he worshipped God through music (95:1). But what characterized David's devotion was not just style or time of day or place of worship. It was the posture of his heart. David was devoted to God Himself, not just to the act of seeking Him. This set him apart from the king before him and the people around him, and it's a model for us today.

Daniel provides another example of biblical devotion. Exiled from Israel when Babylon captured the Jews, Daniel spent much of his life as a Babylonian authority figure. Even in exile, he made a point of keeping God first in his heart and life. It was this devotion—praying to the Lord three times a day facing the temple—that resulted in his being thrown into the lions' den (Daniel 6). Daniel prayed often and intentionally because he loved the Lord God, even when he knew that love would cost him everything.

A more recent example of devotion is the famed Puritan preacher Jonathan Edwards. Edwards was a theologian whose work in the eighteenth century was rooted in a rich walk with God, and that work shaped American church history. He made a constant practice of reading and meditating on God's Word. He described the impact of meditation in his memoirs: "I seemed often to see so much light exhibited by every sentence, and such a refreshing food communicated, that I could not get along in reading; often dwelling long on one sentence, to see the wonders contained in it; and yet almost every sentence seemed to be full of wonders."[2] His love for

the Word and discipline to pursue God through reading, meditation, and prayer changed the course of his own life, his community
in Massachusetts, and eventually the country through the spiritual
revival of the First Great Awakening.

John Wesley, an Anglican minister who in the 1700s founded
what eventually became the Methodist church, led a life characterized by passion for the gospel and personal holiness. In his notes on
the Old Testament, he gave instructions for how to use the spiritual
disciplines to grow in devotion to the Lord.

> If you desire to read the scripture in such a manner as may
> most effectually answer this end, would it not be advis-
> able, 1. To set apart a little time, if you can, every morning
> and evening for that purpose 2. At each time if you have
> leisure, to read a chapter out of the Old, and one out of
> the New Testament: if you cannot do this, to take a sin-
> gle chapter, or a part of one. 3. To read this with a single
> eye, to know the whole will of God, and a fixt resolution
> to do it. In order to know his will, you should, 4. Have a
> constant eye to the analogy of faith; the connexion and
> harmony there is between those grand, fundamental doc-
> trines, Original Sin, Justification by Faith, the New Birth,
> Inward and Outward Holiness. 5. Serious and earnest
> prayer should be constantly used, before we consult the
> oracles of God, seeing "scripture can only be understood
> thro' the same Spirit whereby it was given." Our reading
> should likewise be closed with prayer, that what we read
> may be written on our hearts. 6. It might also be of use, if
> while we read, we were frequently to pause, and examine
> ourselves by what we read, both with regard to our hearts,
> and lives. This would furnish us with matter of praise,
> where we found God had enabled us to conform to his
> blessed will, and matter of humiliation and prayer, where

we were conscious of having fallen short. And whatever light you then receive, should be used to the uttermost, and that immediately. Let there be no delay. Whatever you resolve, begin to execute the first moment you can. So shall you find this word to be indeed the power of God unto present and eternal salvation.[3]

Time with God always has a purpose. Contrary to what we see on social media, it's not just to fill up on the Word or start the day right. The goal of time *with* God is worship *of* God.

In many Western churches, worship is what we do before a pastor's sermon on Sunday. While singing songs can be an expression of worship, songs are not the sum total of worship. Etymologically, *worship* means to "attribute worth to" the Lord (or whatever you are worshipping). God is the most valuable, worthy person we will ever know. Yet we often attribute more worth and value to sleep, social media, and friends than we do to Him. Our worship is naturally revealed through our daily habits and behaviors. The things we think, say, read, watch, and do reveal what we're worshipping. For example, if we attribute more value to sleep than we do to God, we'll cut Bible-study time short for those extra 15 minutes of rest. If we attribute more worth to popular approval than we do to Christ, we'll spend so much time on the right #coffeeandjesus photo we'll lose sight of what we learn in Scripture. But if we want to go deeper with God, the key isn't more Bible tabs or the right set of hashtags—it's a heart that attributes worth to *Him.*

CULTIVATING A HEART OF WORSHIP

What does a heart of worship look like? The simplest way to find out is to look at how worship is described in Scripture. The patterns and words of the Old and New Testaments give us a picture of worship that bends our hearts toward true devotion. These actions and attitudes can transform our time with God. Scripture gives us vivid descriptions of a worshipful heart, as shared in the passages below. I would encourage you to read these verses in context to get a bigger picture of worship and the heart that pursues it.

A worshipful heart...

- Ascribes glory to God and rehearses His goodness (1 Chronicles 16:29).

- Emphasizes His holiness (Psalm 99:1-5).

- Changes our posture and leads us into humility (Psalm 96:6).

- Recognizes idols for what they are and does not attribute worth to anything but God (Daniel 3:28).

- Is led by the Spirit and based on God's truth (John 4:24).

- Brings an offering. In the Old Testament this was an animal, in the New Testament it is our bodies, to be used for God's glory (Romans 12:1).

- Remembers that God is and always will be God and that He is both approachable and awesome (Hebrews 12:28).

- Lays down earthly priorities to recognize God's glory, honor, and power (Revelation 4:10-11).

Worship changes everything. It is led by God's Spirit (His specific leading to our hearts) and founded on God's truth (His living Word). When worship is the focus of our hearts, Bible study isn't boring and prayer isn't painful. A worshipful heart naturally desires the things of God. And if desire is half the distance to a thriving spiritual life, cultivating this desire through heartfelt worship is always worth our time.

DRAWING NEAR IS NOT ALWAYS EASY

Worship is essential to a devotional life that lasts beyond the morning hour. But worship doesn't always come easy. Even when we have the desire, the busyness of our lives makes a morning watch difficult. My 17-year-old-self did not experience this. Drawing near to God in my prayer closet was pretty simple; I could wake up and pray without interruption. I could spend as much time in study or prayer as I pleased. But it's been more than a decade since that season, and my time with the Lord looks very different now. I have two little girls who don't believe in sleeping past 6:30 a.m., and even when they do, packing devotional time, a workout, and writing into the two hours before they awake is a tall order.

When I first became a mom, I struggled with this transition. Even though my quiet time changed a lot when I left my parents' home, it was still something I could control. Now it was interrupted, shortened, and "ruined" because of the appearance of my first daughter. How was I supposed to know God apart from a daily 30-minute time with Him? This was all I'd ever known. How could I go deeper in the Word and my walk when my time with Him was so limited?

My transition to motherhood taught me an important truth about pursuing God: *What Christ cares most about is that you come to Him.* There is no rule in Scripture telling us we can only approach God in the morning. There is no biblical principle that designates 30 minutes as the magic amount of time to spend. God wants us to know Him and, by knowing Him, be known *by* Him.

The season of life we're in can change the contours of our devotional lives dramatically. Early in my career, my commute forced me to become more flexible, and my devotions often took place on my lunch break. And in those early days of first-time motherhood, knowing Jesus happened in 10-minute readings at my dining room table while I nursed, 30 minutes of listening to the Bible on audio while I drove, and written prayers before bed. If I had remained bound to a to a particular means of knowing God, I never would have approached Him at all. The means had to change, but the end remains the same: seeking Christ through His Word and prayer.

We have to be flexible and open-minded in our devotional life. When what was meant to be a joyful relationship becomes a source of guilt and duty, how it must grieve God's heart! But like anything, flexibility can also be taken too far. If we become so flexible in our devotion to God that our study of the Word becomes shallow, or we start depending on Christian celebrities or the latest Christian living book to tell us who God is, our spiritual growth will be hindered. Devotion to God is a dance of dedication and grace. As we dedicate ourselves to knowing God and put effort into our relationship with Him, He gives us grace for our growth.

GROWING UP IN FAITH

Both of my daughters cut their first teeth before they were six months old. By the time they actually reached six months, they were eating like toddlers. Geneva, my younger daughter, can put away as much food as a grown adult—at eight months old! She still loves her bottle, but milk alone will not sustain her.

Geneva would get along well with the author of Hebrews, who told believers in the early church that the goal of following Christ is to grow up: "Anyone who lives on milk [elementary Christian teaching], being still an infant, is not acquainted with the teaching about righteousness. But solid food is for the mature, who by constant use have trained themselves to distinguish good from evil" (5:13-14). We mature in faith by "constant use" of God's Word. We grow in strength, wisdom, and security by constantly approaching

Him, even when circumstances are less than ideal. Spiritual depth and maturity never happen by accident. They are always the product of intentional exposure to the heart and Spirit of God.

Digging into God's Word when you struggle to understand it is hard, but remember: You're not the only one showing up. God rewards those who seek Him (Hebrews 11:6). And it is through the Bible—both Old and New Testaments—that God has chosen to reveal Himself. My goal as an author is not to get you to read more of *my* books (though I appreciate that you are), but to urge you to read the actual Word of God. Reading what Christian authors say about God is still secondhand exposure. You need to read about Him firsthand. You need to see Him through the Word He inspired, the chapters and books that tell us who He really is. As the author of Hebrews put it, to do otherwise is to live on "milk" and to remain perpetually "not acquainted with the teaching about righteousness."

Perhaps you've tried knowing God through the Bible—whether in the morning or on your lunch break or during a 3:00 a.m. nursing session—but you're not getting very far. Even when you pick a book of the Bible to study, get out your notebook, and start reading, everything around you battles for your attention. You end up looking for an easy verse to apply and call it a day. If this is you, you're not the only one struggling! Some of us even wrestle with guilt when our devotions don't look the way we think they should. We see ideal quiet times on Instagram and think, *I need my coffee and ten colored pencils before I can read my Bible today!* Thirty minutes later we're bustling around trying to clean up the house so we can make coffee so we can sit in the armchair so we can study…instead of coming to God without all the trappings. There's a beautiful freedom in simple reading and prayer. Don't let false guilt over your time with God keep you from sitting at His feet. Choose instead to fight for your relationship with the Lord.

This fight will not be easy. The things that prevent us from drawing near are often those harmless, productive distractions: answering an email, checking social media, cleaning up a room. But distraction is only one of the things preventing us from going deeper. I've found there are four common disruptors women encounter as soon as they sit down to seek the Lord:

1. Uncertainty

You don't know what to read, where to start, or how to study. Lack of focus sabotages your time with the Lord from the beginning. To counteract uncertainty and approach God with intention, choose a book of the Bible to study each month. Use a reading plan. Decide what passages you'll read each day of the week and write them in your planner. Find something that works for you to get you in the Word itself, not just a devotional. By determining what you'll read beforehand, you won't flip mindlessly through pages and default to familiar passages you've read before.

It's especially helpful if you take a year or two to read through the entire Bible chronologically. Many Christians have never attempted this, and it's not that difficult. All you need is a chronological breakdown from a site like BibleGateway.com, and many Bibles have reading plans in the back, by the concordance. Don't worry about time frames—just move through the plan each day.

2. Distraction

The second morning watch disruptor is *distraction*. We are a distracted generation, and social media doesn't help. If you always have to have your phone nearby, focus will be difficult. Having the option of the entire Internet at your fingertips will always be tempting when you encounter a tough passage in Scripture.

We beat distraction by knowing exactly how we are going to

spend our time (by setting the intention or plan beforehand) and by focusing on who is meeting us there (Almighty God!). When we forget these things, we start looking for alternatives to consume our minds and quell the boredom we might feel when we encounter tough Bible passages. When we repeat this pattern over time, our spiritual lives remain surface level.

Prevent distraction by putting your phone away during your time with God. I say "time with God," because that is precisely what this time is. We're not talking about mere Bible study or simply reading words on a page; this is time *with God.* Let's not search the Internet or look at Facebook during these intimate moments with our Creator. Put the phone in a drawer, set a timer if you need to, and focus for the minutes you have.

3. Inconsistency

Remember how desire plays a huge part in our time with God? Desiring His presence is key to consistency. We are consistent in the things we enjoy. Inconsistency happens when we let uncertainty and distraction characterize our time with God. What is enjoyable about a half hour spent trying to focus and sit still? Not much! This is why so many people stop coming to the Lord on a daily basis.

To become more consistent in your study, *set a lower bar*. Big goals don't work when you're already struggling with consistency. Instead of meeting God every day for an hour, choose three days of the week and a flexible time to meet Him. Remember, what matters is that you come. It would be better to have three deeper times spent in the Word than seven short, shallow sessions that keep you from knowing Him intimately.

4. Depth

Last but not least, as we talked about earlier, a big struggle for modern Christian women seeking to know God better is a lack of depth. Because we lack focus and are distracted and inconsistent, we default to quick studies or devotionals. These give us a surface knowledge of Scripture and thus a surface experience with God. And because going deeper takes time, it's usually the first thing to go when our schedules get busy. But if we truly want to live the overcoming life and want to experience the living water Jesus promised the Samaritan woman, we have to take time to go deep in study and prayer.

It's uncomfortable to acknowledge these weaknesses in our time with the Lord. It's hard to admit we have a problem with distraction or depth. Yet this is the impetus to change. It is time to do a one-eighty. It is time to stop looking at the Bible for quotes and application and instead look at it as a means to know the living God.

DON'T WAIT FOR PERFECT

Don't wait for coffee or the perfect Bible. Set aside your phone; you can take a cute Bible picture later. Within the pages in front of you is everything you need to know about the God who made you. And each time you expose yourself to the Word, you're dealing a blow to your spiritual enemy. He can fight—and win—against those whose knowledge of God is limited and whose experience with Him is perpetually shallow. But he cannot have victory over a woman whose life is grounded in God's Word.

The quest for the perfect quiet time might have begun with good motives, but it misses the point. Worship is the goal of our time with God, and it is through worship that we become women of spiritual substance, women who can withstand the trials and difficulties of life in a fallen world. Our exposure to God through His Word and prayer determines how we grow up in faith. It's a journey. But God gives us grace for growth, and we should do the same for ourselves. What matters is that we come to Him.

As we open the Word and allow God's Spirit to do the work in our hearts, we're drawn nearer to God. This simple act of coming to worship is a statement of faith: We believe God shows up as we show up. We believe He is faithful. We come, bringing our brokenness and exchanging it for His overcoming power. This exchange can only happen if we make meeting Him a habit.

Coffee and Jesus are great. But at the end of the day, all you really need is Jesus. Don't wait for the coffee—just come to Him.

WHAT YOU CAN DO TODAY

1. If you don't know where to start in your study, pick out a Bible-study reading plan from a site like YouVersion or BibleGateway. Choose one that fits your current study level. If you're a new believer, a simpler, smaller book like 1 John would be a good place to start. If you're a more seasoned believer, start with something more challenging that you may not have read before, like Ezekiel or Isaiah.

2. Assess your own quiet time habits. Do you fall for the lie that things have to be perfect before you can spend time with God? Are you distracted five minutes in? What changes can you make to cultivate a deep relationship with God in this time?

3. Take a moment to think about your attitude toward God. Do you worship Him? If not, begin praying daily for a heart that worships and affirms His character. If you're not sure where to start, choose a characteristic of God we see in Scripture and tell Him how you appreciate this about Him. This is called *adoration*, and it invites our hearts to worship.

PART TWO

SKIRT LENGTH AND BIBLE TRANSLATIONS: OVERCOMING LEGALISM

The sun peeked over the watery horizon and sent beams skipping across the lake. I gazed at it while I wiped down a table. As a waitress in a diner near my childhood home, I spent a whole summer watching the sun rise over the water. I never tired of it.

But I *did* tire of something else, something I spent my whole summer trying to ignore: my coworkers' foul mouths. Anyone who works in food service knows that bad language comes with the territory. I started working outside the home at 15, so it wasn't as if I'd never heard someone swear before. But I was zealous in my young Christian faith and determined to be "set apart" (Hebrews 7:26), so whenever my coworkers would take the Lord's name in vain or drop an F-bomb in my presence, I *made sure* they knew it shouldn't happen again. By the end of the summer, everyone in the diner knew they shouldn't swear around me. Mission accomplished.

But what *did* I accomplish by demanding unbelievers clean up their language? I look back and wonder. As an outspoken Christian, I was one of the few people of faith my coworkers encountered. Based on my demands, they could easily infer that the gospel was more about not swearing than following Jesus Christ. My personal commitment to pure speech could have easily been misconstrued as a requirement to approach God. My coworkers learned a gospel…but one that demanded they clean up their act before coming to Jesus.

Teenage me showed my coworkers Christianity. But the Christianity I showed them was legalistic, adding requirements to gospel grace. Legalism is adherence to law even when Jesus has given us freedom through His blood. Legalistic worldviews say we must dress, talk, and behave in a certain way in order to earn God's favor (or at the very least, not lose His approval). Essentially, we must follow the rules.

Rules make sense to me. I am the oldest of six homeschooled children and naturally type A. My parents have always been very balanced, but because we were raised at the cusp of the homeschool movement—in a rural area of Michigan—my parents thought they had no choice but to involve us in the available homeschool culture. While this served us well in many ways, it also exposed me and my siblings to our first taste of legalism.

As a student who often felt left out and uncool, I grasped for a culture in which I could excel. Legalistic Christian culture fit that bill. I latched on to the rules with ardor—even when my own parents didn't create or enforce them. These rules gave me a sense of superiority: Even though I couldn't be cool, I could judge those who had hurt me. I could hold them up against my personal convictions and find them wanting. Instead of dealing with the hurt of being *left* out, I *lashed* out—using Scripture to support my ungodly attitude.

The particular brand of legalism my family was exposed to in the homeschool world was what most people are familiar with: strict boundaries for behavior beyond what Scripture says. Instead of going on dates, which could lead to sexual temptation and sin, girls and boys "court." Instead of listening to secular music, which could contain crude or vulgar lyrics, Christian music is the only permitted genre. The goal of these rules is admirable: to pursue purity. But when a man-made rule is elevated to the level of divine command, you're looking at legalism.

Legalism takes many forms. Most people associate it with long skirts, long hair, purity rings, and chaperoned dates, but the other extreme is also true. When someone says it's "uptight" or "legalistic" to refrain from swearing, to wear a suit to church, or to sing hymns—as if these things prevent a true relationship with God—that is another version of legalism. You can be just as legalistic about tattoos and trendy church services as you can be about dating and modesty. Legalism is any action added to the gospel in order to please God.

So my no-swearing law may have been respected by my coworkers, but it didn't tell them much about God. All it revealed is what most people already believe to be true: Following Christ is about following rules. Even my own teenage adherence to special rules wasn't done out of love for God so much as it was done for fear of His holiness. While God is indeed holy, using my own efforts to become more holy—and forcing others to be the same—missed the whole point. God gave us a Helper, the Holy Spirit, to guide us, and *He doesn't come with a set of rules!* He comes to help us live out the abundant life Jesus promised (John 10:10).

Legalism is man's shortcut to holiness. But like most shortcuts, it doesn't accomplish God's intentions.

HOW LEGALISM PLAYS OUT

In John 4, Jesus articulated what it takes to live a life that honors God. We touched on this in the previous chapter, but it's worth revisiting. Jesus told the Samaritan woman, "A time is coming and has now come when the true worshipers will worship the Father in the Spirit and in truth, for they are the kind of worshipers the Father seeks" (verse 23). Jesus didn't say, "The true worshipers will look and act a certain way." He cut to the heart of what worship is: a heart pointed toward God.

At the time Jesus met the woman at the well, there were over 600 different Judaic ordinances. Many of these aren't in the original Torah, the law given to Moses by God. In the "silent period" between the close of the Old Testament and the start of the New, Jewish religious leaders added to God's original law (which was meant to keep Israel in relationship with Him and point to the coming Messiah). They set up *rules around the rules* to help themselves be holy. But over time they forgot which rules were God's and which were man's. The result? A self-righteousness that so disgusted Jesus, He rebuked them for it (Matthew 23:1-39).

I never would have called my teenage rules "legalism." I thought of them as guidelines for good behavior. I knew that some parents and churches had more rules than others, and I had dozens of rules for myself. But as I matured in my faith and learned how to follow God's leading, I saw the results of legalistic upbringing play out again and again. Boys and girls I grew up with became men and women who didn't want anything to do with Jesus or the rules they thought He required. But many of the rules they resented were never articulated by Jesus Himself. In a sad twist of irony, the parameters created to make them "good Christians" sent them running away from God.

This pattern is not new. Legalism always ends in one of two ways: self-righteousness or hedonism. Whether we end up exalting our own good behavior or rejecting it in order to please ourselves, it starts with the same problem: a small view of God.

THE "RIGHT" WAY
TO BE A CHRISTIAN
IS TO FOLLOW THE
SPIRIT ACCORDING
TO THE WORD.

BIG RULES, SMALL GOD

When my siblings and I were teens, our parents suggested we refrain from dating in high school. It wasn't a hard and fast command, but a strong suggestion based on their own experience, knowing most high school relationships didn't last. We complied with their guidance (something I'm very grateful for), and then when I turned 18, I was asked out on a date.

I didn't know what to do. *What's the rule for these situations?* I wondered, my face flaming as I tried to figure out an answer. Naturally, I chose the most normal response: I told the guy he needed to call my dad, handed him a handmade business card (not joking!), and bolted up the sidewalk to my car. Smooth.

When I told my dad what happened, he laughed out loud. "Why did you do that?" He was incredulous. "I never told you a guy had to call me before you could go on a date with him! If he's a decent guy, I trust you."

My parents' initial rule was given out of love and wisdom. But I took their instruction and created extra rules for myself—ones my parents *never even gave me*. We do the same thing with God's law. We take the law of love, which was meant to keep us in harmony with Him, and add an extra burden to His commands. Then, when the burden becomes too heavy, we blame God for being unreasonable and run from His grace.

Running from God because of man-made rules is a pattern as old as humanity. We see this play out clearly in Jesus's interaction with the Pharisees and Sadducees, the Jewish religious leaders responsible for arresting Jesus before His crucifixion. You would think that the Pharisees (from the Hebrew "Set Apart Ones"[1]) would embrace God's Messiah. After all, they knew God's promise of a Savior better than anyone else. But for all their talk about God and His holiness, the Pharisees' view of Him was actually quite small. God, to the religious leaders, was concerned with the rules that made people *look good*, no matter what was going on inside. The religious leaders added hundreds of regulations to God's original commands in the name of honoring the Lord, but these regulations missed God's ultimate mark. They ended up serving the law, not serving God.

That's what legalism does: It limits God, minimizes who He is, and blinds us to His true work. Legalism presents Him as caring more about outward actions than the heart *behind* those actions, even though Scripture shows us a God who is most concerned about the motives of our hearts (1 Samuel 16:7).

JESUS BREAKS THE "LAW"

Jesus faced legalism throughout His ministry. The legalism of Israel's religious leaders was evident throughout the Gospels in their conversations with Him, specifically on the topic of the Sabbath (Matthew 12; Mark 2; Luke 6; 13; John 5). Intent on protecting God's law, the leaders targeted Jesus. But Jesus was bringing the law back to God's original intent. We see these two worldviews collide in John 9, where Jesus took on the religious leaders in a debate about working on the Sabbath. How Jesus dealt with their accusations shows us how to confront legalism in our own hearts and communities.

The story opens with a man born blind. This is significant because Jewish leaders taught that the Messiah would fulfill the prophecies of Isaiah 35:

> Then will the eyes of the blind be opened
>   and the ears of the deaf unstopped.
> Then will the lame leap like a deer,
>   and the mute tongue shout for joy (verses 5-6).

Jesus's healing of the blind man was fulfillment of Messianic prophecy, and the Pharisees likely knew this. The fact that the healing took place on a Sabbath broke *scribal* law, but it fulfilled God's promise.

Jesus expressed the urgency of this healing to His disciples: "As long as it is day, we must do the works of him who sent me. Night is coming, when no one can work. While I am in the world, I am the light of the world" (John 9:4-5). With this in mind, we see how intentional Jesus was in this healing. He *knew* He was "breaking the Sabbath"—at least according to Judaic scribal law—and He did it anyway.

Everyone was astonished by the blind man's healing. His neighbors and friends couldn't believe it. Before long, the Pharisees heard about what Jesus had done. The healed man was brought to the religious leaders to testify against Jesus and report what occurred:

> They brought to the Pharisees the man who had been blind. Now the day on which Jesus had made the mud and opened the man's eyes was a Sabbath. Therefore the Pharisees also asked him how he had received his sight. "He put mud on my eyes," the man replied, "and I washed, and now I see." Some of the Pharisees said, "This man is not from God, for he does not keep the Sabbath" (verses 13-16).

Honoring the Sabbath—God's mandated day of rest each week—is one of the Ten Commandments. But the scribes created detailed statutes for all of the Ten Commandments, with a long list specific to Sabbath observance. These statutes forbade carrying a "burden" (even one as light in weight as a dried fig), harvesting food (including handfuls of grain—Matthew 12:1-2), and transporting a tailor's needle in one's jacket. They also forbade healing. In his commentary on John, William Barclay shared just how far the Pharisees went in their legislation:

> It was forbidden to heal on the Sabbath. Medical attention could be given only if life was in actual danger. Even then, it must be only such as to keep patients from getting worse, not to make them any better…Clearly the man who was born blind was in no danger of his life; therefore Jesus broke the Sabbath when he healed him.[2]

The scribes and Pharisees took God's broad principle—the command to set aside the first day of the week to honor the Lord—and made it a heavy, legalistic burden. They also missed the entire point of God's Sabbath: to rest, worship, and celebrate godly community. Could not all these things be accomplished through healing the sick?

But these extra rules had even more drastic consequences. Only a hundred years before Jesus's birth, over a thousand Jews (including women and children) were slaughtered by a Greek military force because they refused to defend themselves on the Sabbath. (This is recorded in the historical book of 1 Maccabees 2:32-38.) The Sabbath became both more and less than God intended it to be. What God created to bless Israel became instead a bondage, and Jesus would have none of it.

The blind man in John 9 was in a tough spot. The Pharisees accused him of covering for Jesus. Trying to trap Jesus for His "sin" of healing on the Sabbath, they interrogated the healed man until he confessed his belief in Jesus's power, saying, "Nobody has ever heard of opening the eyes of a man born blind. If this man [Jesus] were not from God, he could do nothing" (verses 32-33).

The Pharisees were enraged. Because they believed things about the Sabbath that God never taught and because—in their minds—man-made additions had become God's law, Jesus's pro-phetic, miraculous healing was offensive to them. Jesus *couldn't* be the Messiah because in their eyes, He was breaking God's Sabbath. It didn't make sense!

It didn't make sense to the Pharisees, but it made a lot of sense to God. The religious leaders had forgotten which rules were writ-ten by God and which were written by man. They had forgotten the spirit and purpose of God's law. Healing someone on the Sabbath physically and spiritually captures the very heart of God's sacred rest. But the Pharisees couldn't see this. As the healed man stood before them, it was the Pharisees who were blind.

Because God is holy, He has given us a standard of moral purity by which to live. This "law" looks different today than it did for Israel, but the same spirit remains in both. We can't earn peace with God through the law; we choose holiness because we have His peace! But when we add to this law of love, we put a burden where none existed. We become blind to the beauty of God's grace. Like-wise, the Pharisees were blinded by their own legislation, which Jesus pointed out when they found and confronted Him:

> "For judgment I have come into this world, so that the blind will see and those who see will become blind." Some Pharisees who were with him heard him say this and asked, "What? Are we blind too?" Jesus said, "If you were blind, you would not be guilty of sin; but now that you claim you can see, your guilt remains" (verses 39-41).

Though the religious leaders followed every detail of the scribal law, that's not what God was after. He didn't care that they wore the "right" clothes, prayed elaborate prayers, or kept people from violat-ing their terms for Sabbath. Their hearts were far from Him.

THE YOKE IS EASY

If you grew up in an environment that required certain clothes, types of music, dating rules, and the like, letting go of the rules can feel like letting go of Christianity. Accepting Christ's offer of freedom—freedom to follow His Spirit into holiness—feels like a big risk. How do we know what the Bible condemns and what we're free to do in Christ? We'll get to that in a minute, but first, let's look at Jesus's heart for all His followers:

> Come to me, all you who are weary and burdened, and I will give you rest. Take my yoke upon you and learn from me, for I am gentle and humble in heart, and you will find rest for your souls. For my yoke is easy and my burden is light (Matthew 11:28-30).

The word *yoke* was a euphemism for "teaching." Jesus was saying His teaching—in contrast to the heavy burden of legalism—is *easy*. Following Him is not complicated. The Pharisees made it complicated. Some churches today make it complicated. But God wants us at rest in His Spirit and from that place of restful trust, to walk out our faith with confidence. This was what Jesus meant in John 15 when He said, "Remain in me, as I also remain in you. No branch can bear fruit by itself; it must remain in the vine. Neither can you bear fruit unless you remain in me" (verse 4). Unless God leads us into true heart change, external behaviors have no eternal merit.

A few days ago I saw a blog post entitled "Men Prefer Debt-Free Virgins Without Tattoos." The author of the article, a Christian woman, argued that today's women are saddled with so much college debt, they cannot give their best to their future homes and families; that our sexually promiscuous culture has infiltrated even the lives of Christian women; and that Christian women are disobeying God by getting tattoos. The author stated that between debt, loss

LEGALISM IS ALWAYS THE PRODUCT OF *MISINTERPRETED* SCRIPTURE. WHEN WE LOOK AT THE ACTUAL TRUTHS GOD HAS FOR US, WE FIND FREEDOM LEADING TO HOLINESS.

of virginity, and tattoos, Christian women are making themselves undesirable to Christian men. The author used Scripture to back up her points, emphasizing God's demand for holy living because He is a holy God. And I agree: He *is* a holy God. But He is also merciful.

Legalism always starts with a little truth, which is why it's so convincing. The Bible does advise us to make wise use of debt and not to go into debt foolishly or impulsively (Psalm 37:21; Proverbs 28:8; Matthew 25:27). And God is clear that sexual promiscuity is outside His will and evidence of living in the flesh (1 Corinthians 6:18; 1 Thessalonians 4:3). But the author of the blog post took these biblical truths and expanded on them, presenting her opinion as God-ordained law.

When we look at Scripture, we find a different story. The Bible does not expressly forbid going into debt; in Matthew 18, Jesus told a parable depicting a lender relationship. Debt is not ideal, but in some circumstances it is unavoidable and can definitely be paid off with wisdom and diligence. Loss of virginity, too, may occur from living a promiscuous lifestyle—but it may also occur at the hands of rape or sexual abuse. And for those who *have* missed the mark in God's design for sex, there is redemption for all those who are in Christ (2 Corinthians 5:21). As for tattoos, the only mention of them is in Leviticus, where they are forbidden in the context of pagan idol worship (Leviticus 19:28). This law was very specific to the culture in which Israel lived at the time.

This blog post illustrates an important point: Legalism is always the product of *misinterpreted* Scripture. When we look at the actual truths God has for us, we find freedom leading to holiness. I suspect it would surprise the author of that blog post to learn that when I married my husband, I was a debt-free virgin and I had no tattoos, but he wasn't drawn to me because of the rules I followed; he was drawn to me because we shared a love for Christ. My virginity and financial choices were the outflow of my love for Him. Jesus didn't die only for debt-free virgins without tattoos, or for people of a certain denomination, or for people who get *redeemed* in Hebrew tattooed on their wrists. He died for *everyone*. And even after we accept Christ, our righteous choices should come from a desire to walk in peace with Him.

Legalism starts when we take biblical *principles* (use money wisely) and expand them to universal *commands* (it's a sin to go into debt). While some things—such as sexual purity—*are* commands from God, they are commands colored by grace. Only in Christianity do we have hope for restoration. Jesus redeems it all: broken sexuality, overwhelming finances, or anything else we face this side of heaven. Legalism brings condemnation. Grace brings hope.

LIFE UNDER GRACE

Yesterday Adeline, my two-year-old daughter, was not being very cooperative. "No!" she screamed from the crib. "No No No!" Tears and snot were streaming down her face as she refused the one way she could get out of time-out: obedience.

"If you are ready to be respectful and kind, you can come out."

"No!"

Five times I went into her room and offered her the choice of obedience or staying in time-out. Five times she rejected the offer. I was getting frustrated. How could she not see the benefits of doing what I asked? She'd be free to play, eat snacks, and spend time with her sister. But in her toddler rage, nothing was rational.

I came into her room one last time and said nothing. I just pulled her across the bed into my arms and held her angry little form. A few minutes passed, then I felt her body relax. She looked up through tearful gray eyes. "I sorry, Mama."

Like my toddler, we resist obedience even when it results in blessing. God could condemn us for our stiff-necked behavior, and we sometimes do receive consequences for our poor choices. But it is God's *grace*—the open arms of Jesus on the cross, every day of our walk with Him—that calls us to repentance, redeems us, and restores us. It is His grace that teaches us what is right and wrong.

In legalistic Christianity, God is a father who can never be pleased. His holiness is unapproachable, and we often feel as if we can't measure up in His eyes. Apart from Christ, that's true. But it was *God the Father* who sent Jesus on our behalf. And it is *God the Father* whose grace makes us holy people. It is God's grace that changes us. His mercy draws us to repentance.

Life under grace can't be narrowed down to a list of rules. Following the Spirit's leading means no two lives will look the same. In the body of Christ are women who saved themselves for marriage and women whose sexual pasts have been completely redeemed. There are people who grew up knowing the Bible and people who read it for the first time at age 32. There are people who only wear skirts, and people who wear shorts and tank tops. Following Jesus is not about doing whatever we want, but about *doing whatever the Spirit leads us to do.*

ALL YOU HAVE TO DO IS FOLLOW HIM

If you grew up in a Christianity of law and regulation, this may be a foreign or scary thought. May I encourage you? God is on your side! He wants your righteousness, but it's not up to you to accomplish it. If you follow His leading, righteousness will naturally flow from your life. You will make good clothing choices. You will handle your finances well. You will honor your sexuality. *All you have to do is follow Him.*

Letting go of legalism is a journey. For years, I had to process unconscious guilt—which is never from God—over what I thought was the right way to be a Christian. But the "right" way to be a Christian is to follow the Spirit according to the Word. When we live under condemnation, we naturally condemn others. But when we live under grace, we are quick to offer compassion. We celebrate those growing in faith alongside us, not comparing how they work out their salvation to how we're working out ours. Like the Samaritan woman, we are free to worship—not according to tradition or regulation, but in Spirit and in truth.

WHAT YOU CAN DO TODAY

1. Don't skim the questions today. Get a notebook and write out some thoughts: Have you lived under the burden of laws God never gave? How has this affected your view of Him?

2. Do you follow "Christian" behavior out of guilt and fear brought on by a church or family member? Why or why not?

3. Do a little research into who the Pharisees were. You can find information on a Bible study website like GotQuestions or BibleGateway. How could people who knew that much *about* God miss God's Messiah? In what areas of your life are you missing God's heart?

6

THE COURAGE TO TRUST: BATTLING ANXIETY AND OVERWHELM

Hunched over my keyboard, the familiar tightness began in my chest, creeping to my shoulders and my neck. The phone rang again, and I cringed. It was the most stressful season for my job, with phone calls streaming in every few minutes, each with a different request. The work was tedious and detailed, required constant flexibility, yet demanded I create structure (structure that my customers often ignored). The job was everything my personality was not.

I'd never considered myself an anxious person. I equated anxiety to fear, and I'm generally very confident. But in that season I learned just how anxious I really was. The constant changes at my job made me feel helpless and out of control. For this type A woman, this meant frustration on a daily basis. The stress became so intense, my shoulders developed scar tissue from the tension. My chiropractor worked on my back for a full year to alleviate the pain. I would go home from work exhausted and negative, dreading the next day of phone calls. I thought I was immune to anxiety—but I wasn't.

As the conversation around stress and anxiety has gained visibility, hundreds of books have been written to address it—both Christian and secular. I've read some of these books. I've implemented their advice. But I've discovered it doesn't matter how many deep breaths you take, how organized your schedule is, or how relaxing your nighttime routine is. Apart from Christ, there is no lasting solution. Most of what is written about anxiety helps us live with the *effects* of anxiousness, but to *overcome* it? This seems impossible.

REST FOR OUR SOULS

If you've lived with anxiety for most of your life, the thought of overcoming it sounds like an unrealistic dream. Yet this is exactly what Jesus promised His disciples. And it's not just what He promised; it's what He *empowers* us to embrace.

Jesus's promise is not as simple as "pray about it" or "have enough faith," two of the common platitudes Christians throw at anxious believers. There is no quick fix for a soul-deep struggle. Though it's not easy and certainly not quick, Jesus never makes a promise He won't bring to fruition. Here are a few of the things He says about anxiety and finding peace:

- "Come to me, all you who are weary and burdened, and I will give you rest. Take my yoke upon you and learn from me, for I am gentle and humble in heart, and you will find rest for your souls. For my yoke is easy and my burden is light" (Matthew 11:28-30).

- "Peace I leave with you; my peace I give you. I do not give to you as the world gives. Do not let your hearts be troubled and do not be afraid" (John 14:27).

- "Therefore I tell you, do not worry about your life, what you will eat or drink; or about your body, what you will wear. Is not life more than food, and the body more than clothes? Look at the birds of the air; they do not sow or reap or store away in barns, and yet your heavenly Father feeds them. Are you not much more valuable than they? Can anyone of you by worrying add a single hour to your life?" (Matthew 6:25-27).

Most Christian teachers focus on Jesus's commands: "Don't be troubled" and "Don't worry." But the command to refrain from worry is always coupled with Jesus's compassion, as seen in Matthew 6. "Do not worry about your life," Jesus says. "Because this life is about *so much more* than the temporal things. I will provide for your daily needs, just as I provide for the smallest creatures." In other words, overcoming anxiety is not about white-knuckling, emotional self-control but about choosing trust in Christ's provision.

My own anxiety wasn't confined to one season. I remember sitting in our Virginia apartment, eight months pregnant with our first daughter, tears streaming down my face. In less than two weeks we were moving to a new state, a new city, and a new community where I knew only one person. I called every birth center and hospital within a 30-minute radius of the Pennsylvania town to which we were relocating. All of them were full to capacity. "I'm sorry," the receptionists said. "We just don't have room for any more October clients." That familiar tightness crept into my chest, I struggled to breathe, and the tears dropped between my fingers. *Where will I have my baby?*

WHERE IS THE LINE BETWEEN TRUSTING GOD AND *DOING* SOMETHING?

In that season I often returned to the story of Jesus's birth as detailed in Luke 1–2, identifying deeply with Mary's uncertain road to Bethlehem. I was on my own journey to first-time motherhood, and there was definitely "no room at the inn"! As our moving day drew closer, every anxious thought was a struggle. I begged for God's intervention, to show us what to do and where to have our baby. *Where is the line between trusting God and* doing *something?* I wondered.

TRUST AND ACTION

"Come to me, all you who are weary and burdened, and I will give you rest" (Matthew 11:28).

Those words of Jesus are so simple, yet so full of power. We love how they look on a Pinterest quote, but do we put our hope in them? Do we really believe Jesus gives us rest? If we did, I'm not sure we'd see the church plagued with the amount of anxiety we see today. We aren't sure of the balance between trust and action, so we choose action over trust. God does want us to take action—Jesus's words indicate this—but the action we take usually isn't what God intended.

I struggled with this balance as we left Virginia with no birth plan in place. In a final search of desperation, I googled "home birth midwives." I had not planned on a home birth, but it seemed like my only option. With only five weeks to spare (which actually ended up being only two since Adeline came early), I located a midwife who was willing to take my case. It seemed like God's provision, but I wasn't sure. I was still anxious about all the unknowns, but there was nothing I could do except trust the path God was leading us down. I needed rest, and Jesus said there was only one way to get there: *Come to Me.*

Overcoming anxiety is the daily choice to *come*. When we feel weary, burdened, and overwhelmed, changing our schedules and habits will help, but these will not bring us lasting victory. Being present and letting go of perfectionism will help us make great strides, but these actions will not cut to the spiritual root of anxiety. Anxiety is overcome when we make the choice to trust God *more* than we trust our emotions. We do this by stepping through the anxiety and bringing it to the throne of grace over and over and *over* again.

Over and over and over again I brought my fears to God the week we moved to Pennsylvania. I resigned from my five-year career in higher education on a Saturday. We packed our moving truck on a Sunday, moved into our new apartment on Sunday night, and five days later, Adeline was born.

If I had known just how fast it would all happen, I never would have left my bedroom in Virginia. But what *grace* that God protected me from this knowledge. Through the uncertainty of that season, I learned how to submit my anxiety to Him. The God who cares for sparrows was not about to leave me in my moment of need, but my mind and worried heart needed to hear that truth.

My choice to trust Him wasn't a onetime event. It is a daily, hourly, moment-by-moment walk of faith—a choice to give my burdens over to Him instead of letting them take me captive.

CHOOSING TRUST OVER FEAR

Choosing trust is not a magical cure. Victory is not defined by never feeling anxious. And in some seasons, and for some people, additional intervention will be necessary. But God has promised that rest is available, rest produced by faith in Him. Rest for our souls is found in choosing trust when trust doesn't make sense. We

REST FOR OUR

SOULS IS FOUND IN

CHOOSING TRUST

WHEN TRUST DOESN'T

MAKE SENSE.

can do this not because our circumstances are ideal, but because our God is trustworthy.

I'm making this sound simple. And Jesus Himself answered anxiety in very simple terms. But He never said it would be *easy*. Many of us bring baggage to our walk with God, baggage that wears us down, holds us back, and keeps us from the deep spiritual life we long to experience. Choosing to trust God is a process, especially when your mind and heart are trained to live afraid.

In my seasons of stressful work and an uncertain baby delivery, I could not trust that my job would change. I could not trust that I'd get an ideal birth experience. Neither of these things were guaranteed to me. My hope and security *had* to be in something outside my circumstances—and so do yours. Choosing trust is the first step, but what are we trusting? What do we believe in if changed circumstances aren't a guarantee?

We *trust* in the character of Almighty God.

And we *believe* for His saving power on our behalf.

In a world of uncertainty, He is unchangeable. Hebrews 13:8 says, "Jesus Christ is the same yesterday and today and forever." In Malachi 3:6, God promises about Himself, "I the LORD do not change. So you…are not destroyed." What a promise! We are *not destroyed* by our circumstances, our relationships, or our future because *God does not change.*

God's unchangeability, omnipresence, and unfailing love make Him worthy of our trust. The biblical battle plan against anxiety is counterintuitive: Rather than focus on beating anxiousness and worry, we lock our eyes on who Jesus is and, in so doing, find victory.

BATTLING ANXIETY DAY BY DAY

A few years after my stressful job and Adeline's arrival, Josh and I moved to Michigan for his engineering job. It seemed like a dream come true: Josh would no longer be working crazy, long hours, we'd be near my family, and we could finally buy a house. Josh had been working at his new job for nine months when we found out we were expecting our second baby, Geneva. We also found the perfect Michigan home. I still remember that Monday night at the bank, signing papers for the mortgage.

Josh left for work as normal the next day. Two hours later, he pulled into the driveway, his shoulders sagging as he slowly ascended the steps of our new home.

He had been let go from his job.

The sudden loss of Josh's work ushered us into a two-month season of job hunting, using all our savings to pay the new mortgage and our midwife, and leaning on God's provision like never before. I spent many early mornings weeping over my Bible, battling anxiety the way I knew best: on my knees. But choosing trust didn't end when my Bible closed; I had to choose trust every single hour. I'd commit my fears to the Lord one minute and be crying over my kitchen sink an hour later.

In that season anxiety was my default setting. It was where my heart wanted to stay. I felt as though I was living a repeat of our life two years prior. But in the midst of our struggle, God reminded me of a secret advantage: I had seen His faithfulness before.

What seemed so unfair—a pregnancy marred by stress and uncertainty—was God's preparation. Realizing this became my weapon against anxiety. The things we'd gone through two years before were benchmarks of God's faithful nature. We had tangibly seen His provision, and we had confidence we would see it again. But I had to preach this to myself in order to believe it.

In overwhelming situations, simply reading Scripture is not enough. We need to hear God's promises in every way possible. The

GOD'S KINDNESS

AND PAST

PROVISION ARE

A TEMPLATE

FOR HIS

FUTURE ACTIONS.

truth of God is most thoroughly absorbed when audibly spoken. So when anxious feelings crowded my heart and threatened my peace, I would say aloud, "God has always been faithful to me, and He will continue to be faithful to me. My God will provide all our needs." Over and over I repeated how God had rescued us in our move to Pennsylvania; how He provided my first midwife, Shirley; how He blessed us with our Christian landlord, an affordable home, and a wonderful church community, not to mention a seamless delivery. God was faithful before. God would be faithful again. His faithfulness—not my changed circumstances—was my sword against anxiety *every single day.*

It's a simple practice—rehearsing God's faithfulness. It's hard to choose. Our emotions tell us to dwell in fear, to try to figure it all out on our own. But we do not give up, because our God does not give up on us. God's kindness and past provision are a template for His future actions. Not only do we have a glimpse of His heart through our *own* past experiences, we have the entire Word of God as further proof we can trust Him. He hung a rainbow in the sky to show Noah His faithfulness. He gave Abraham and Sarah a child in their old age, just as He'd promised. He parted the Red Sea to free Israel from an oppressive master. And He sent Jesus as the Second Adam, the one who would bless all nations, to bring all people to God through Himself.

FIGHTING FOR PEACE

The overcoming life is a process. Just as wars are made up of many battles, some that end in defeat, the overcoming life is not marked by constant perfection. Victors are people who keep fighting even after a defeat has occurred. Victors are the ones who, like soldiers and generals, assess the loss, recalibrate, and join the battle once again.

As we fight to overcome anxiety (or anything else, for that matter), its negative presence must be replaced with a positive one. Conquering anxiety is great, but what will fill its place? In the well-known passage of Isaiah 26, the prophet gives us the answer: peace. And not just regular peace, but *perfect peace.* I love the way the Holman Christian Standard Bible expresses it: "You will keep the mind that is dependent on You in perfect peace, for it is trusting in You" (verse 3). The terms here are active, present verbs indicating constant forward motion. According to this text, peace isn't something that just happens to us. It's the product of *intentional dependence* on God. If you're an American, dependency is a big no-no. We are a people of rugged individualism. *Inter*dependence takes a back burner to *independence*… and just plain *dependence*? We run the other way! In our world, she who is most self-sufficient is most celebrated.

Being self-sufficient is great when everything is under control. But when circumstances change and life turns hard, responsibility becomes anxiety. The simple truth is this: We are not sufficient on our own strength. We can't possibly control every outcome, predict the future, or plan for the worst-case scenario. Whether we recognize it or not, we're dependent on God. Too many of us don't recognize this. With our mouths and minds we say we trust God, but our anxious hearts reveal the truth. We believe it's all up to us to secure the best job, find the perfect man, be a model Christian, and produce godly children. The pressure is driving us insane. We tell ourselves, "If I could just find work-life balance" or "If my kids were just a little older" or "If I could just spend a little more time in the Word," the stress and overwhelm would abate. But life only gets busier, and the solution to our run-ragged days still sits before us, untouched.

WE BELIEVE IT'S ALL
UP TO US TO SECURE
THE BEST JOB, FIND
THE PERFECT MAN, BE
A MODEL CHRISTIAN,
AND PRODUCE
GODLY CHILDREN.
THE PRESSURE IS
DRIVING US INSANE.

DEPENDENCE ON GOD

I get personally frustrated by vague spiritual terms, and I'm guessing you do too. So here's what dependence on God looks like, practically.

- Dependence is *acknowledging* our inability to control, predict, and secure the outcomes we want for our lives.

- Dependence is *cultivating* an appropriate reverence for God's goodness and ability (the fear of the Lord).

- Dependence is *choosing* to trust God before we see any change in our circumstances (believing in faith).

- Dependence is *walking* in faith that God is completely good, and believing that His love guarantees the best outcome for our situation (even when it's not on our time frame).

I'm writing this on a plane from San Francisco to Chicago. I'm convinced that the Chicago O'Hare airport has a personal vendetta against me, because of the 20-plus times I've flown through it, I've been delayed almost every time. Before this particular trip I actually asked our small group and my mentors to pray specifically for no connections to be missed. But after sitting on the San Francisco tarmac for two hours, that prayer was not answered the way I'd hoped.

Situations like these make me both anxious and angry. What's wrong with wanting to get home to my babies? Why couldn't God make the O'Hare airport do something right *just once*? I'm not happy with my circumstances. My desire for control and order leaves me helpless in this airline seat.

But maybe that's right where God wants me.

No, I won't be home on time for church. Josh will have to

HOW CAN WE TRUST
HIM FOR OUR ETERNAL
DESTINY AND *NOT*
TRUST HIM WITH OUR
PRESENT FEAR?

minister to the college students without me. I won't see my daughters for another full day, and I'm missing my friend's baby shower. But what feels like a big mistake to me is already known by Jesus. In this moment I have a choice: I can depend on my own understanding, or I can lean on His.

> Lean not on your own understanding;
> in all your ways submit to him,
>> and he will make your paths straight
>>> (Proverbs 3:5-6).

You don't have to like your circumstances to depend on God in the midst of them. Faith and happiness are not synonymous. But you can have perfect peace and consistent victory when you take the step of faith in God's goodness. He sees you. He already knows your situation. He is present with you. *You can trust Him.*

FIGHT BACK WITH FAITH

God's trustworthiness is the strength behind our battle against anxiety. Every weapon we use against anxiety must start with who He is, because only then do we invite an objective perspective and power into our circumstances. Jesus is the most trustworthy person who exists. Think about it: How can we trust Him for our eternal destiny and *not* trust Him with our present fear?

Hebrews 11 is often called the "Hall of Faith" chapter of the Bible because it highlights people of great trust in God. One of those people is Abraham, whose faith in God was "credited...to him as righteousness" (Genesis 15:6). I often think Abraham must have been anxious and overwhelmed at the thought of never having an heir. He must have struggled even more when God *promised* him an heir and then it didn't happen for ten more years! Yet in circumstances

WE CHOOSE

FAITH ANYWAY.

primed for anxiety, Abraham chose trust, and because of this faith God declared him righteous (Romans 4:1-12).

Faith is a word we throw around a lot in Christianity, so here's a working definition: *trust in God's goodness and ability.* When we call ourselves Christians, we're saying we believe God is both good and able—not just eternally, but presently as well.

Because anxiety is a response to fear or lack of control, it is not possible to simultaneously be in a state of trust *and* be overwhelmingly anxious. Can we be tempted toward anxiety? Absolutely! The temptation is not the problem, nor is it a sin. But a consistent lifestyle of anxiety paired with no effort to submit these emotions to the Lord or believe His promises points to a problem with trust. Those of us captive to anxiety need a fresh perspective on God's will for our emotions. We also need a deep appreciation for Christ Himself. Our hearts cannot be simultaneously set on Jesus and bound to the situations we want to fear and control. When we concern ourselves more with outcomes than with God's overcoming power, our emotions get the best of us. But everything changes when we acknowledge our anxious tendencies, recognize the temptation at hand, and consciously turn our emotions over to the hands of God.

This is a daily, hourly practice. It's a choice: a choice to consistently entrust our overwhelming circumstances to Him—even when we have to do it over and over again. But we do so in faith that He's going to show up. We fight anxiety in faith that His will is our peace and His heart is our freedom.

Your feelings may not change immediately. Sometimes they won't change at all. This doesn't mean you don't have faith; it just means you must continually choose faith even in the midst of anxiety. Have you ever considered that true courage is choosing faith in the face of fear? It takes courage to battle anxiety with the truth of God. Women of God have an inner strength not because they are never tempted to control or feel afraid and anxious, but because they fight back.

We live in a fallen world with fallen natures. And if we've spent years habitually giving in to anxiety, it's going to take time in the Spirit to achieve consistent victory. We choose faith anyway. We believe that God is both willing and able to help us, even when we don't feel His presence or don't see signs of His working. As Oswald Chambers so succinctly said, "God's silence is not His absence." If faith is hope in what is not yet seen (Hebrews 11:1), true faith will step out emotionally even *before* the feelings change. Victory is achieved through consistently walking in step with Jesus, and a battle precedes any visible change.

As long as our spiritual enemy exists, we will face emotional battles. But the difference now? We *know how to fight.* Each time we embrace our identity in Christ—not our identity in anxiety—we're taking a step of trust. We're stating belief in God's goodness and ability.

We are fighting *fear* with *faith*.

WHAT YOU CAN DO TODAY

1. We may not overcome anxiety and feelings of being overwhelmed quickly; many of us have to make a daily choice to trust. But you can start by making a separation between the *feeling* of anxiety and your Christian identity. You are not an anxious person. You are an overcomer in Christ who battles anxiety.

2. Fight fear with faith. Each time an anxious thought comes into your mind, recognize what's happening. Stop, address the thought, and pray it back to the Lord. Commit each and every anxious moment to Him in a continual conversation about your fears.

3. Find counseling, mentorship, and support. Fear and anxiety cannot be overcome alone. This may be a combination of church and medical support, but be sure to plug yourself into a strong community of believers who can walk beside you on this journey. More on this in chapter 9.

7

A TIME TO WEEP: GRAPPLING WITH GRIEF

Each year I read through the Bible from Genesis to Revelation. This practice lands me, by the middle of the year, in the book of Job. Job is not my favorite book; in fact, until my Bible-reading plan forced me to read it, I avoided studying it whenever I could. The back-and-forth between Job and his friends, Job's stalwart defense of his innocence, and the cosmic battle for Job's life all confused me greatly. Job is not an easy read, and it can't be narrowed down to a few quaint application points.

One of the most disturbing things we see in the book of Job is the sheer magnitude of grief and loss. Everything that Job could lose, he lost—except his wife, who told him to "curse God and die" (Job 2:9). His children, wealth, and well-being were taken from him in the blink of an eye, and the only thing he had left was life itself. Even Job didn't see this as a great tradeoff, often saying he wished he hadn't even been born (Job 3:11).

I read Job again this year, once again dreading the trudge through two weeks of its chapters. But this time new truths leaped off the page. This time I came away thinking, *Perhaps this book isn't about application. Perhaps this book was included to show us it's okay to grieve, to be full of questions and pain and disappointment. Maybe Job is here not to enhance a systematic theology but to show us God's kindness for the brokenhearted.* This thought transformed how I read the book of Job, but it also transformed my view of other passages. The Bible is full of passages depicting grief, loss, and disappointment. The saints of ages past experienced these emotions *just like we do.* Reading their accounts helps us form a full picture of who God is in the face of grief.

OUR GRIEF, GOD'S PURPOSE

I'm in the stage of life where all my friends are married and having babies—at least some of them are. In the last year I have watched six of my friends walk through a miscarriage, some multiple times. I have watched others wait month upon month, year upon year, through the pain of infertility. As a friend observing from the sidelines, I've felt helpless. Holding someone's hand as she weeps her loss, bringing her a meal, sending a card…these efforts of mine seem like a drop in the bucket compared to the waves of grief rolling over her. Walking beside my friends has driven me to understand how Christ meets us in our loss, and not just how to *face* grief, but how to *experience it* as He did.

My friends have faced infertility and loss, but grief takes many forms. When Josh lost his job, I grieved not just the absence of a steady income but the change to our lifestyle. The insecurity of being pregnant, with a new house, in a rural area without a huge market for engineers left me grasping for why God allowed our situation. Well-meaning people would cheerfully offer encouragement:

"He'll have a job in no time!" "Just think how much time you have together!" Their desire to cheer us was well-meaning, but their words ricocheted off our pain. Beneath Josh's job loss was an iceberg of fear and uncertainty—a nearly empty savings account, no health insurance, and a baby due in three months. Telling us it would all "be okay" wasn't helpful; we needed grounding in a deeper truth.

But the grief of Josh's job loss paled in comparison to the sudden death of a family friend. I remember looking at the picture framed at his funeral: It was his wedding photo, a picture of him and his wife standing on a grassy hill, holding hands as he leaned back in laughter. It was the way we knew him—laughing. But now there is a void: a void in our church, in our hearts, and in our lives.

We need the truth of God in such moments. It's what we all need when we are grieving.

Job, too, was frustrated by empty platitudes. Though his friends joined him in his suffering and attempted to empathize, they had a discouraging view of suffering. Not only did they fail to encourage him, they cross-examined Job for unexposed sin, insinuating he was to blame for his dire circumstances. Job's story teaches us many things, but one thing is for sure: Our fellow humans can never fully empathize with our loss. Even the best of them can't fill the gaping hole in our hearts. We need something—Someone—more.

In Job's day, Jesus had not yet come to earth. The only way to be reconciled to God was through animal sacrifices. There was a separation between God and man that had yet to be bridged. We see Job's longing for something more as he cried out from the midst of his grief:

> I wish that someone might arbitrate
> between a man and God
> just as a man pleads for his friend (Job 16:21 HCSB).

In that day, if a man needed an advocate in court, his friend could stand in for him. This friend would represent the accused and defend him before the judge. Job longed for someone to intercede for him in this way before God, someone to present his case, to ask God why.

What Job could only hope for, we have today. Jesus is our high priest, always interceding for us and our pain. Through Him, we have access to God Himself. We can pour out our hearts, our loss, and our grief, and be heard:

> Since we have a great high priest who has ascended into heaven, Jesus the Son of God, let us hold firmly to the faith we profess. For we do not have a high priest who is unable to empathize with our weaknesses…Let us then approach God's throne of grace with confidence, so that we may receive mercy and find grace to help us in our time of need (Hebrews 4:14-16).

We often quote Hebrews 4 in the context of sin—Jesus can empathize with our weakness because He Himself was tempted as we are. But Jesus also experienced the weakness of grief. When His friend Lazarus died, Jesus—the Son of God, the Alpha and Omega, *the Resurrection Himself*—wept. He grieved the effects of death on His friend. In the Garden of Gethsemane, Jesus grieved the road to the cross. He was, as Isaiah 53 says, "A man of suffering…familiar with pain." But the difference between Jesus's grief and the world's? He knew Easter was coming. Jesus knew He'd *overcome*.

Being Christ-followers gives us a different perspective on loss. It's not that we don't feel the pain; the difference is, as the apostle Paul put it, "You do not grieve like the rest of mankind, who have no hope" (1 Thessalonians 4:13). We might not *feel* hopeful, but we *have* a hope that outlasts death. We have the promise of an eternity free from pain, suffering, and grief.

Last year one of my dear friends walked through a season of inexplicable loss. A health scare that resulted in major surgery, the death of her father to cancer, and her mother struggling with the loss—Michelle was hit by what can only be described as a "fiery ordeal" (1 Peter 4:12). In that same season, she celebrated the wedding of her sister and—most importantly—the long-awaited adoption of their family's baby son.

Joy and sorrow were mingled in Michelle's life. As I watched her walk through this season, I noticed she never denied the grief she felt. She was always honest about it. But she was still full of joy because she did not grieve as if she had no hope. Though Michelle never would have chosen those circumstances for herself, her grief glorified God to those watching her walk through them, just as the apostle Peter said it would:

> In all this you greatly rejoice, though now for a little while you may have had to suffer grief in all kinds of trials. These have come so that the proven genuineness of your faith—of greater worth than gold, which perishes even though refined by fire—may result in praise, glory and honor when Jesus Christ is revealed (1 Peter 1:6-7).

WHEN EVERYTHING TURNS TO DUST

Back to Job: About halfway through the book, Job responded to his friends' second round of critiquing, begging them to see his side. After crying out for pity, Job seemed to turn inward and declared a truth that timelessly endures: "I know that my redeemer lives, and that in the end he will stand on the earth" (Job 19:25).

At the very last—the last of our money, our security, our family, our *life*—who is still there? In the dust of our possessions and achievements, our Redeemer is alive. He is there, never forsaking, overcoming our pain with His presence. At the very end of ourselves and our hope, Jesus is still standing. This is how people can endure trials that don't make sense. His promise never to leave or forsake is an eternal promise, the kind of promise even death cannot destroy.

CASE STUDIES IN GRIEF

The women highlighted at the beginning of this book knew a little bit about grief and loss. Dinah lost her honor, her virginity, and her expectations for her future in the patriarchal culture of her day. The Samaritan woman grieved the loss of *five* husbands, and if the divorces were because of barrenness, her heartbreak was only multiplied. But Dinah and the Samaritan are not the only pictures of loss in Scripture. There are other women who have walked this road before us, giving us a model for facing our own fiery trials. The following characters show us not just what grief looks like, but who God is in the midst of it.

Hagar (Genesis 16)

God promised Abraham and Sarah a child. When a child did not come, Sarah took it upon herself to suggest her servant, Hagar, as a surrogate.

Hagar had no choice in this matter. She went from household slave to master's concubine overnight. Caught in the crossfire of faithlessness, Hagar became a pawn in her mistress's plan to acquire an heir.

Naturally, this arrangement created conflict in Abraham's household. Hagar took pride in her new position and her ability to bear a child. Sarah resented Hagar deeply. With Abraham's blessing to do "whatever you think best" (verse 6), Sarah mistreated Hagar so terribly the slave ran away into the wilderness.

When we read this story, we usually focus on the co̶̶̶̶̶̶
by lack of faith. But let's look at it from Hagar's point of v̶
moment. She came to this situation powerless, was manipulat̶
her mistress (who goaded her husband into using her, then resente̶
the result), and was mistreated enough to consider the wilderness
a better option, even in an extremely vulnerable state. I picture her
walking through the desert on aching, swollen feet, exhausted and
thirsty, terrified for both herself and her baby. If she survived the wilderness, where would she go? Women had no support system outside of marriage, and Hagar wasn't married in an honorable sense;
she was at best a "secondary wife." She was simply a means to an end.

Hagar grieved the loss of security, identity, and a future. She
grieved the potential loss of her life. She couldn't go back, and she
could hardly go forward. But there, in the midst of Hagar's pain,
God met her:

> The angel of the LORD found Hagar near a spring in the
> desert; it was the spring that is beside the road to Shur.
> And he said, "Hagar, slave of Sarai, where have you come
> from, and where are you going?" (verses 7-8).

God often greets us with questions. This is a curious habit, con-
sidering He already knows everything. But the questions He asks
force us to acknowledge our deep need.

Hagar didn't answer Him. There really wasn't an answer. "I'm
running away from my mistress" (verse 8) said nothing about *where*
she came from because she never belonged in the first place. And
she didn't bother to say where she was going because she probably
didn't know.

Deep loss has this effect. Our purpose loses clarity in the throes
of grief, and it is incredibly hard to remember both who we are and
where we are going. In this wilderness of pain, God doesn't expect

own strength. He simply meets us in the

n before she even cried out. It is no won-

God who sees me…I have now seen the

, verse 13).

s grief, God was the *one who sees*.

Hannah (1 Samuel 1)

We meet Hannah in the first chapter of 1 Samuel. She was one of two wives, and though her husband was kind and loving, Hannah was bullied by the other wife because she couldn't bear children. This provocation usually occurred on the way to the tabernacle, and when we meet Hannah, that is exactly where she was.

Hannah's grief was deep. Every day she was reminded of the child she could not have. On her knees in the tabernacle, we see her anguish poured out to God:

> She was deeply distressed and prayed to the LORD and wept bitterly. And she vowed a vow and said, "O LORD of hosts, if you will indeed look on the affliction of your servant and remember me… but will give to your servant a son, then I will give him to the LORD all the days of his life" (verses 10-11 ESV).

I find it beautiful that Hannah's bitterness was not directed at her husband or toward the cruel second wife, Peninnah, but *to the Lord*. Hannah didn't deny what she was feeling. As she told Eli the priest later, she was "a woman troubled in spirit" (verse 15 ESV). But rather than contain her bitterness and anger, Hannah poured out her soul to God (verse 15 ESV). She didn't care how foolish she looked (Eli mistook her for being drunk, after all) or what the people around her thought; she brought every ounce of grief and pain and poured it out to the Lord.

The image of "pouring out" is an interesting choice in this

context. In the list of offerings and sacrifices documented in the books of Leviticus and Numbers, there is one that receives much less attention than the others: the drink offering. Drink offerings were made of strong wine (a symbol of rest and joy) and were poured out with the rest of a sacrifice. No part was set aside for the priests' consumption. When wine was offered to God, all of it was laid at the altar. Drink offerings were also never offered by themselves. They always accompanied a sacrifice.

I think of Hannah's grief as a drink offering, poured out alongside her sacrifice—including the future sacrifice she would make in giving up Samuel to God. Rest and joy were not something Hannah was experiencing. But Hannah poured herself out anyway; all the rawness, the anger, and the loss. Hannah withheld nothing from God. She left it all at the altar.

Hannah's walk through infertility is one many women can identify with today. How she dealt with her barrenness gives us an example for processing our own grief with God. Rather than let her infertility drive her *away* from the Lord, she let it drive her to Him. She was completely honest with God. She held nothing back, not even the child God would one day give her. God doesn't always answer us the way He answered Hannah, with a child in her arms, but she is still a model for our own grief in infertility. "In due time" (verse 20 ESV) Hannah's prayer was answered, and she "bore a son, and she called his name Samuel, for she said, 'I have asked for him from the LORD'" (verse 20 ESV).

For Hannah's grief, God was *the one who answers*.

Naomi (Ruth 1–4)

We usually focus on the story of Ruth when reading this book by her name, but Ruth's mother-in-law gives us another picture of grief. After leaving her homeland due to famine, Naomi settled in the foreign land of Moab. It was here her sons married Moabite women (forbidden by Israel's law), and it was here that Naomi's husband died. Grief upon grief caused Naomi to name herself "Mara," which means *bitter* (Ruth 1:20). But through this short book we see Naomi comforted and cared for by her daughter-in-law Ruth, given purpose and hope through the redemption of Boaz, and eventually become a grandmother when Ruth and Boaz have their child, Obed (the grandfather of David!). For Naomi, God *was the one who restores.*

Dinah (Genesis 34)

We first encountered Dinah at the beginning of this book, but let's revisit her story. Dinah was the only daughter of Jacob. You'd think her father and brothers would have protected her from selfish, violent men. But Dinah was attacked and taken into Shechem's home with no interference from Jacob, and her brothers weren't aware of what had happened to her until later.

Dinah was probably a virgin when Shechem took her. At the hands of a selfish man Dinah's future was dashed to pieces. She was now "used goods," unwanted, an object of either sexual desire or sexual shame.

Dinah's grief must have been immense. And because so much is left unstated in the biblical narrative, we're left wondering if anyone cared for Dinah. Her brothers were too caught up in the family honor to consider how Dinah felt. We don't know where her mother, Leah, was. Jacob was completely silent. How heartbreaking must it have been to be abandoned by everyone close to you in your time of greatest vulnerability?

Dinah's story ends with Jacob protecting himself. There is not a word about her destiny. Not a word about God's response. We know He did not endorse what happened to her—we know it was the product of a man's selfish will. But the silence of God in this account is something many of us can relate to when we are in the throes of grief. For Dinah and her grief, God—at least based on the record we have—was silent.

The Samaritan Woman (John 4)

Grief was no stranger to the woman at the well. She'd been either widowed or divorced *five times*. There's a chance she was infertile, like Hannah.

Grief and loss of love were her story. Yet here, at the well, sat a Jewish man who cared. A man who asked about *her*. A man who saw into her soul, beholding everything she'd ever done, and still offered her a better life. In her simple testimony, "Could this be the Messiah?" the Samaritan woman's voice reverberated through time. On this ground where Dinah had been violated, in this land where Hannah wept, Hagar wandered, Sarah abused, and Naomi returned home empty-handed, a Savior stepped in.

Just as Jesus stepped into the Samaritan woman's grief and loss, He steps into ours. He entered into our pain when He went to the cross, and ever after He is interceding for us before the Father (Hebrews 7:25).

I often think about how God answered so many women in these narratives, but Dinah's story ends in silence. Where was He? Why don't we see a happy ending? I had a chance to wrestle with these questions when, during the writing of this book, I broke my leg in a soccer game. Our entire world stopped. I went in for surgery and left with a plate and eight screws below my knee. In one night, I went from an active mom of two to an incapacitated woman unable to even *dress* myself. In the midst of the excruciating pain of the surgery, my autoimmune disease continued to flare up, covering my face in an ugly, painful rash. It took the little I could already do and cut that in half. I had never felt so abandoned by God.

I battled God's silence in those weeks. I have prayed for healing of my disease for years. While some progress has been made, it is largely the same—sometimes worse than before. So when my broken leg took away the normalcy of life, I faced a greater grief—one I'd been ignoring. *God does not hear me,* I wept. *He is silent to my pain.*

But something I learned in those two months of inability (and the months to come of therapy and slowness) is that silence—in our lives or in Dinah's narrative—does not mean God is absent. In the silent periods we must choose to trust who God has proven Himself to be in every other story we know. God is just. God is kind. God is present. God is love. This was Dinah's hope, and it's ours as well.

Our grief is *known and carried.* Our loss is not pointless. In the lives of our biblical predecessors we have a template for God's movement with humanity. He did not abandon His women before, and He will not abandon us now.

HE BINDS UP
THE BROKENHEARTED

During the span of time in which I wrote this chapter, my friend Bekah watched her baby boy be born, go through two heart surgeries, and three weeks later pass into the arms of Jesus. I got the news that Jace was with the Lord in the middle of Bible study. I went to my room to be alone—to cry alone. I hadn't met my friend's little son, but as a mother to two little girls, a small echo of her grief gripped my heart. Bekah has shared openly about her family's journey through the grief and loss they're experiencing. But rather than let the nightmare drive Bekah *away* from God, it has driven her to even deeper faith. With her permission, I'm sharing something she wrote a month after Jace's homegoing:

One month—it has been one month since you left this earth. While we are learning and trying to find our "new normal," the fact still remains that we can't help but feel like something is always missing. I am clinging on to the fact that you are happy and healthy in heaven with a God whose love is unconditional. I do believe that one day I will see your beautiful face again. But it hurts so bad to think of all our hopes and dreams that we had for you are lost. Our family will never be the same and will be forever changed, all because of you.

One thing God has been teaching me through this entire journey is to trust Him. Even in those last moments of Jace's life all I wanted to do was hold on to him so tight and not let go. I begged God to spare his life and for him to make it through this. But it was when I finally decided to trust Him with my child's life and the plan He had for him all along, that I finally let go and said, *Okay, God. You can take him. I trust You.* It was that moment when I had peace. I had peace that God would take care of my son, that he would not have to be a fighter anymore, that he would be getting the new heart we prayed for, that he would never have to experience the heartache and darkness of this world. God did answer all of our prayers, just not in the way we expected.

When you ask us how we are doing—we are taking it one day at a time, one moment at a time. And trusting God, trusting that this is the journey He has chosen for us. We miss Jace. We miss him every single day, every hour, every minute.

Christian grief does not require pretending everything it okay. It does not mean we cease to feel, to hurt, to wonder if the void will ever again be filled. And we won't always understand why our loss occurred in the first place. Christian grief is all the pain and loss *plus* the presence of a loving and faithful God. Bekah expressed this when she noted, "God did answer all of our prayers, just not in the way we expected." God was—and is—present with their family. And He is present with you.

YOU ARE KNOWN AND CARRIED

"The Lord lifts up those who are bowed down," said the psalmist. "The Lord loves the righteous" (Psalm 146:8). When you are bowed down beneath the weight of your grief, broken by the depths of your loss, and hurting in ways no human being can truly identify, the Lord your God lifts you. This image reflects the maternal aspect of God's character: His gentleness, patience, and compassion. In seasons of grief, we need this comfort. We need a gentle and compassionate God.

Our trials and suffering can often make us feel very alone, but the Word of God shows us women who walked this path before us in faith, trusting that they were *known* and *carried*. Your own pain may echo that of Hagar, or Hannah, or Naomi, or Dinah, or the Samaritan woman—or perhaps Bekah or Michelle. Women across the ages have faced things none of us would choose. But the difference for women of God is *God Himself.* In the loneliest and most painful moments of our lives, He will not forsake us. He is a God who enters into pain, who is "close to the brokenhearted" (Psalm 34:18) and who "binds up their wounds" (Psalm 147:3).

WHAT YOU CAN DO TODAY

1. If you are walking through a season of grief, think about the women described in this chapter. With whom do you most identify? What did they do that you can imitate in your own walk with God?

2. Ask yourself, "Have I been holding back my heart from God in this season? Am I angry at Him? Too overwhelmed to even begin pouring out?" God can handle your disappointment. He can even handle your anger and confusion. Bring it all to Him. For reading, I suggest starting in the book of Job or Psalms.

3. If you aren't in a season of grief, is there someone in your life who is? Think of three practical ways you can support, encourage, and bless them in this season. It could be bringing them a meal, taking them to get coffee, or just sitting with them at their home to fold laundry or hold their hand.

8

USED GOODS: REDEEMING A BROKEN SEXUALITY

I stumbled upon the book at a garage sale.

At 12, I didn't know what sex was. It was before Internet porn became readily accessible, and I wasn't in an environment where I heard too much about sex. But I knew enough to realize the book wasn't something I should read.

That book opened a door to years of sexual fantasy and addiction. As a Christian teen, I went through cycles of anger, depression, apathy, and victory. Each cycle made me more desperate to get free from the bondage of sexual sin. Each failure sent me spiraling into a crisis of faith. *Am I even saved if I keep on sinning like this? How could God still love me if I scorn His grace?*

To make matters worse, the hardest years of my addiction took place during my teens—when I was a member of a girls' drama group focused on purity. To the outside world my addiction to erotica and self-pleasure may have been harmless; I wasn't *actually* having sex. But I knew the truth: My addiction was the same, at its core, as the girl sleeping with her boyfriend.

When I met my husband, our respective sexual histories collided. Though I was still a virgin, I had a thought and heart life scarred by sexual fantasy. He had lost his virginity to a girlfriend before me. We both grew up in Christian homes, knew what we believed, and met at a Christian college. All the *facts* of God were available to us. So where was the victory?

My walk through sexual sin is what made me so passionate about the victorious Christian life. I spent too many years living below God's calling, not understanding the power and forgiveness He offers. As I struggled through my sexual addiction, I was forced to acknowledge what I believed about God. Did I believe He was actually powerful? Actually able? Actually *willing* to forgive and restore? These were the questions I had to face as a Christian caught in sexual sin.

I'm not alone in my story. According to multiple surveys, 20 to 50 percent of women have actively used porn individually or in their relationship.[1] Just as many are addicted to masturbation, like I was, or are engaging in sexual relationships with their boyfriends. And this isn't just in our culture at large—it's a pervasive problem in *the church*. These are women who know about Jesus, and not just about Him; they know Him *personally*. So where is the disconnect?

I had this same disconnect, so I can pinpoint the origin. In my personal experience and in counseling women through sexual addiction, sexual sin is not something they pursued. It all began *by accident*: A book at a garage sale. A pop-up on a website. A manipulative boyfriend. An abusive relative. The initial encounter with sinful sexuality was something that happened, not something they chose.

This wrecked me as a young believer. I felt that God had abandoned me at that garage sale. I couldn't believe He would allow me to find that book in my young, vulnerable state. While I knew I was responsible for the choices I made sexually, I struggled to embrace God's love when I didn't *ask* to be introduced to sexual sin.

Time gives us a vantage point, and as I look back on the past 16 years, I can see how my discovery of that book has been redeemed in a beautiful way. I still don't have a clear answer on why it happened to me, but I know God can provide victory. And not just victory—He can, and does, provide *beauty* to the sexually shamed. But the messages I heard in the midst of my struggle were not enough to free me from my embarrassment and addiction. Being told I was beautiful meant nothing when I knew the truth about who I was and what I'd done. Those platitudes fell flat. I needed more than most female Christian ministers could offer me. I needed real, raw power over sin. And if you're in the middle of sexual bondage, it's what you need too.

THE POWER OF FEMALE SEXUALITY

I may not know why I was introduced to sexual sin, but I know why it happens so often: There is a spiritual target on female sexuality.

The Enemy has been after female sexuality from the very beginning. There is something about femininity that Satan hates with all his being. Perhaps it is the beautiful completion she brings to man's mission. Or maybe it's her status as the deliverer of new life. Perhaps it's the significance of her sexuality blending with man's in perfect marital unity. Whatever the case, I am not surprised to see so many women struggling with sexual bondage. The Enemy is working overtime to tell us lies about sex, such as:

- Sexual sin is a man's problem. You're a freak for struggling with it.

- You can't talk about your sexual issues. No one will be there for you if you do.

- God doesn't forgive sexual sin.

- Your virginity is the sum of your identity.

- Good men don't want damaged goods.

- If you've sinned sexually, you can't have a godly marriage or a good sex life.

- Sex is a duty women fulfill for their husbands.

These lies have a goal: to drive us *away* from God and the sexual freedom He offers and to drive us *toward* shame and further enslavement.

Many women don't understand the nature of their sexuality enough to fight and win. Most of us are in the business of sin management. We are constantly trying to suppress our desires: frantically squashing them, setting up standards and making rules, trying to make it for a stretch of time without sinning. We are crushed when we repeat the cycle over and over again. Recognizing that the Enemy wanted to destroy my sexuality—my God-designed sexuality—put things in perspective for me. But the real change came when I learned my sexuality was not the problem; my spirituality was. The state of my spiritual life had a direct connection to my sexual behavior, and if I wanted to overcome, I had to fight spiritually first.

Fighting spiritually might sound vague, so here's the first thing to know: Sexual struggles are not about sex. They aren't about your body. They're about your spirit. And until you fight back spiritually, you will never gain victory sexually. It is your soul that is under attack, and your body is just the tool to accomplish the Enemy's purposes. He knows that to enslave you sexually, he must deceive you spiritually.

And that's why you have to fight.

Strangely, the fight against sexual bondage isn't about setting more rules. It's about drawing closer to Jesus. The solution to this spiritual battle is to be spiritually grounded in your relationship with God. This is why comfy, "pink fluff" Christianity doesn't free people—it doesn't reach the soul! We need a soul-deep solution to our battle, and that solution is Jesus Himself.

WHAT GOD ACTUALLY SAYS ABOUT SEX

We're all well-versed in the lies about sex, but what about the truth? What does God actually say about our sexuality? God's heart toward our sexuality is revealed in the Bible from beginning to end. We see His directives, His design, and His redemption over human sexuality from Genesis to Song of Solomon to Hebrews. Embracing (and celebrating) our God-designed sexuality requires that we understand it from His perspective.

I was recently watching the movie *How to Lose a Guy in 10 Days*. One of the characters in the movie is known for her weeklong relationships. The character would sleep with her dates the first week, and following these sexual encounters, she would become very emotional, to the point of crying or saying, "I love you." This behavior scared off the men she was dating, leaving her to wallow in the aftermath of yet another failed relationship.

The movie presents this girl as unstable and needy for feeling those emotions after a one-night stand. In reality, these emotions are a natural part of sex. They are supposed to be there! Sex was designed for emotional and physical closeness. If we followed the subliminal messages of *How to Lose a Guy*, we would stifle our emotions, separate sex from our desire for a lasting love, and continue to give ourselves to men who want to use us for physical reasons alone. And sometimes that's exactly what we do.

Sex is not just a bodily function. It involves thoughts and emotions that heighten the sexual experience and are inseparably tied to our minds and hearts. Part of what makes sex so appealing is the sense of closeness we have when we participate in it. This is God's design. God intended sex to be this way, and He created us with the ability to experience it. Being a relational God, a God who guards intimacy with everlasting covenant, the intimacy of sexuality is important to Him.

BE INTOXICATED WITH HER LOVE

Sex is first depicted in Scripture in Genesis 4:1. The writer of Genesis used the Hebrew word *yada*, which means "to know," saying, "Adam *knew* Eve his wife, and she conceived" (ESV, emphasis added). *Yada* is consistently used in the Old Testament in reference to covenant relationship. Marriage, and the sexual relationship within it, is the most glorious example of the intimate relationship God desires with mankind. It is founded on commitment, faithfulness, mutual love, and complete vulnerability. I love this verse from Proverbs that reveals the contrast between illicit sex and marital sex:

> Drink water from your own cistern,
>   flowing water from your own well.
> Should your springs be scattered abroad,
>   streams of water in the streets?
> Let them be for yourself alone,
>   and not for strangers with you.
> Let your fountain be blessed,
>   and rejoice in the wife of your youth,
>   a lovely deer, a graceful doe.
> Let her breasts fill you at all times with delight;
>   be intoxicated always in her love (5:15-19 ESV).

Scattered, streets, strangers: This is the life of a sexual nomad, never committing to the beauty of God-designed love. Marital sex, however, is a reservoir of satisfaction rather than the "scattered springs" of illicit sex. It is a continual fountain, always renewed—not the dark, empty streets of a city. It is a place to rejoice, delight, and be completely intoxicated with love, not overcome with temporary lust. It is security. It is a place where we are free to feel all the heights of emotion that accompany sex, and if we are moved to tears and say "I love you"—like the girl in *How to Lose a Guy*—there is no place for shame.

Granted, there are nights where the experience may not be the best. My wedding night was fine, but not the best sex we've ever had. Sex takes practice, and in a relationship founded on commitment, sex is a journey a man and woman walk together. They are progressively sanctified as they give of themselves with patience, gentleness, and real love—the kind that commits to never, ever leave.

If God designed sex this way, how could we possibly think He wants us to look at it as gross, evil, bad, or dutiful? *God* is the one who celebrates sexuality, and the Enemy has been twisting God's purpose for sex since the very beginning. How do we end up so far from God's design? How can we end up with a sexuality warped by shame, sin, guilt, or duty? It starts by confusing *desire* with *lust.*

LUST VERSUS DESIRE

When God tells us to reserve sex for marriage, He is not telling us to deny the existence of our desires or be ashamed they exist. He, the designer of sex, is revealing to us the blueprint for the most fulfilling sexual relationship we can possibly have.

God's design for sex is based on real, God-defined love. It is good to desire that kind of love. But when our desire for love is reduced to a desire for physical closeness alone, we have missed the point entirely. Sexual sensations are a product of sex—but they aren't the purpose. The purpose of sex is unity (Mark 10:8), service of one another (1 Corinthians 7:1-40), and pure, faithful love (Hebrews 13:4). In contrast, the world's template for sex is based on lust, whether or not they use that word.

Lust is a vague word, usually associated with porn addiction and the modesty conversation. It's been overused in the church, and few of us even know what it means or what the Bible says about it. Interestingly, the church used to use the term *lust* to describe any unholy desire—sexual or not. Only in the last century or so have we shifted to seeing lust as a sexual desire alone.

The Bible supports the concept of lust being any desire that is contrary to God's law. Here are a few things we know about it from Scripture:

- The lust of the flesh and of the eyes belongs to the world (1 John 2:16).

- Lust limits our ability to fight against sin and pollutes our hearts (2 Timothy 2:4,22).

- Lust wages war against our souls (1 Peter 2:11).

- Lustful minds conform us to the world (Romans 12:2).

If we are to fulfill God's will, which is for us to be holy (1 Thessalonians 4:3-8), the fruits of lust cannot be found in our lives. Jesus said only the pure in heart will see God (Matthew 5:8) and that we are not of the world (John 15:19). Our separation from the world occurs when we follow Christ, and every choice we make after following Him is a choice to live up to that identity or to go back to our old ways. If you've battled sexual sin like I have, walking this out is

SEXUAL SENSATIONS

ARE A PRODUCT

OF SEX—BUT THEY

AREN'T THE PURPOSE.

easier said than done. It took seeing what lust actually *does*—to me and to others—for me to get serious about my walk with God and the sexual freedom He offers.

So how do we know the difference between lust and godly sexual desires? Lust is an almost obsessive attention on attaining something. It is not patient or willing to give up its rights. A lustful mind is more focused on its desire than on the consequences of that desire; it is both sensual and insensitive. In contrast, godly sexual desire honors others. The desire may be recognized, but it is not acted on until the appropriate time. It is characterized by love (1 Corinthians 13:4-8).

Lust also satisfies itself first. Lust is focused on satisfying a want that it perceives as a need. The desire becomes so strong, a lustful mind sees what was once a longing as an inalienable right. But godly sexual desire does not confuse *desires* with *needs*. Just because we long for something—even something God-designed—does not mean we get to have it.

Lust takes God's plan for sex out of context. God's context for sex is marriage because sex inside of marriage (when the man and woman love God and each other) is in submission to God and His design for sex. It does not seek the bare minimum but seeks to glorify God by honoring Him and by honoring the other person. Because godly sexuality begins and ends with the Lord, marriage is a safe place for sexual desires to be acted upon and explored.

Perhaps most alarmingly, lust usurps God's authority. Choosing to lust after someone and then acting on it is an unspoken belief in one's own sovereignty. We're essentially saying, "I am god of this area of my life. I will dictate the limits of my own sexuality." We're elevating ourselves above His standard of holiness in the same manner Satan did before he was cast out of heaven (Ezekiel 28:12-17).

Sexual sin is a big deal not because it's a "bigger sin" than others, but because it affects us emotionally, physically, mentally, and spiritually—and when it happens in a relationship, it affects someone else.

"HOW FAR IS TOO FAR?"
IS THE WRONG QUESTION

For most of my sexual journey, I struggled alone. My battle with erotica and masturbation was my darkest secret. I set up strict standards with the guys I dated, knowing my own capability of going too far. Most of my relationships were too short-term for me to face temptation with my boyfriend, but when I began dating someone as weak as myself, things spiraled out of control.

I thought I could separate my sexual issues from my daily life. I was wrong.

My private, spiritual struggle spilled over into my relationships. It became confusing, shaming, and worse—hypocritical. While I never had sex with any of my boyfriends (including Josh), I understand *completely* how "good Christian girls" like me end up doing so.

The Enemy is sneaky. He knows we don't compromise our values without having made decisions along the way that eroded our resolve. No one goes from "I'm saving sex for marriage" to "Forget this, I'll just have sex" overnight. Something has to change in our minds and hearts to bring us to that place. That something is the Enemy's shame. You're probably familiar with this voice:

You've already gone too far. You can't go back now.

God won't forgive repeated sin.

You're too much of a hypocrite for a good man to ever want you.

When we believe these narratives, we give up. We run away from God and His loving heart for our sexuality and go back to the slavery Christ died to end.

Some people try to fix their sexual problems with more rules.

You're looking at the queen of boundaries in dating. I tried every-thing. What I discovered is that the question is never, "How far is too far?" but "Do I really desire to be holy?" Holiness keeps us at peace with our holy God. We are called to be holy, set-apart peo-ple, but when our hearts don't desire what God desires for us, there is no rule we will not break. Physical standards don't work if your heart doesn't love what God loves. And we can't love what God loves if we don't love God.

ACCEPTING GOD'S LOVE
LEADS TO FREEDOM

Loving God was a foreign concept to me for many years. I could grasp an intellectual appreciation, or perhaps a deep gratitude...but love? Emotional, spiritual, whole-person love for God was some-thing I didn't understand.

I began to study what love looked like in the Bible. God's defini-tion of love is founded on sacrifice and commitment, and this affects the entire Christian sexual ethic. To love others by God's design, I had to love God—and to love God, I had to understand what love means *to Him*. I started by reading how He loves us.

- "Can a mother forget the baby at her breast and have no compassion for the child she has borne? Though she may forget, I will not forget you! See, I have engraved you on the palms of my hands" (Isaiah 49:15-16).

- "The LORD appeared to us in the past, saying: 'I have loved you with an everlasting love; I have drawn you with unfailing kindness'" (Jeremiah 31:3).

- "This is love: not that we loved God, but that he loved

us and sent his Son as an atoning sacrifice for our sins"
(1 John 4:10).

God's kind of love is everlasting. It is faithful. And most of all, it
is sacrificial. He sent Jesus to purify us so that we could have a relationship with Him. We see an example of God commanding this
kind of love in Paul's instructions to husbands in Ephesians 5:

> Husbands, love your wives, just as Christ loved the
> church and gave himself up for her, to make her holy,
> cleansing her by the washing with water through the
> word (verses 25-26).

God's love will make us holy. The world's love might temporarily
satisfy, but it can never present us to God unashamed. Sex outside
of marriage is unholy because it upends the very nature of intimacy,
which has always been meant to be enjoyed in the context of covenant relationship. Always. This includes sexual intimacy. Because
God loves us, He designed sex this way, and because God loves us,
He restores broken sexuality and offers forgiveness through the cross.

But many of us struggle to accept God's love for us. This is especially hard for those trapped in sexual sin. We are conscious of our
wrongdoing; so conscious, we have a hard time comprehending
anything but God's judgment toward us. But Christ took our condemnation on the cross, and this includes the condemnation of sexual sin. Until we embrace God's love for us through Christ—until
we accept it, believe it, trust it, live in it—we will not be free.

God so loved us He sent Christ to pay for all our sins, which
includes our sexual sins. God wants freedom for us! But we can't
get there if we don't understand and embrace the gospel: His righteousness covers for our failure, heals our shame, and redeems our
broken sexuality.

PROCLAIMING A REDEEMED SEXUALITY

Redeemed sexuality is sexuality healed by a loving God. God-defined sexuality starts with repentance and ends in redemption.

This kind of hope and restoration exists only within Christianity. Everywhere else we're told to either *hide* our sexuality or *embrace* it, sin and all. But our God takes broken sexuality, reshapes it, and makes something completely new. He buys back what was given away and "clothe[s] [us] with garments of salvation, He has wrapped [us] with a robe of righteousness" (Isaiah 61:10 NASB).

I resonate strongly with the Samaritan woman. When she ran back into the city after meeting Jesus, she announced to everyone, "He told me everything I ever did!" When you've lived in sexual shame, announcing "everything you ever did" sounds more like the stuff of nightmares than cause for celebration. We'll discuss shame in more detail in chapter 11. But it's important to note, for the Samaritan woman, shame's power was broken. It held her no longer—and it no longer holds me. That's why I can write this chapter to you, telling you about one of the hardest, rawest parts of my past, hoping it opens a freedom door in your own life.

CELEBRATING REDEEMED SEXUALITY

God's view of sex is one of celebration.

Celebration of our sexuality requires this kind of daily walk with the Spirit. As we embrace God's love, our desire for sex may not go away, but it can be used as a testament to God's power in us. When we desire sex, we aren't desiring something wrong; we're desiring something God designed. We celebrate with Him when we use that desire as a means to pour out our hearts to God, inviting His presence and power over our sexuality. Our desire for sex can be one of the greatest faith-walks of our lives.

We are sexual beings before and after marriage, and the sooner we acknowledge that, the sooner we will live out God's sexual freedom. Our sexuality has kingdom purpose. Naturally, the Enemy is after it. We fight back by trusting God's love and goodness, even in the face of doubt. We don't allow Satan to hold us captive to our past sexual failures. Instead, we allow the desire for sex to be the good and wonderful thing God designed it to be, neither worshipping it nor ignoring it.

It is never too late for the sexually broken. Redemption is as simple as letting the Man at the well retell your story in gospel terms. It's choosing to live up to the identity Christ gave you. And it's celebrating the beauty of redemption: real sexual healing, undeserved and complete.

WHAT YOU CAN DO TODAY

1. Identify the lies you believe about sexuality. These are often rooted in how sex was taught to you at a young age. List the words that come to mind when you think about your sexuality: *Dirty? Sinful? Shameful? Dutiful?* Compare these words with what we discussed in this chapter. Does your perspective align with God's view?

2. If you are currently living in sexual sin and bondage, it's not too late to make a change. Right now, acknowledge where you know you are grieving God's Spirit. Pray out loud in repentance to the Lord. First John 1:9 promises, "If we confess our sins, he is faithful and just to forgive us our sins and to cleanse us from all unrighteousness" (ESV).

3. Think about what it means to celebrate your sexuality. If you're married, this means actively prioritizing this part of your marriage and discovering any emotional or spiritual sexual baggage that needs to be dealt with. Find a biblical counselor, if necessary, and discuss the issue with your spouse. If you're single, this celebration of your sexuality starts by reframing it in your mind. Go back over the lies and truths about sex in the first discussion question. Then begin to view your desires as an opportunity to worship God, much like the hunger pangs we feel when fasting. It's not easy at first, but as you consistently direct your desires back to the Lord in earnest prayer and cast yourself on Him in dependence, you will see a change in how you view and walk out your sexuality.

9

KNOWN AND WANTED: CULTIVATING A LASTING COMMUNITY

was standing on my alma mater's intramural field as she sneered at me, her blue eyes haughty with contempt. "When you said you weren't good at sports, you weren't lying." She tossed the football in the air and caught it behind her back. I'd been invited to go to the field with several girls from my dorm, and—trying to be a willing participant—I went. Regret and shame battled for first place as I walked off the field. I had been mocked and derided by this girl before, and I was over it. I used to cry when it happened, but now I was filled with rage. *Why do I even try to be friends with these girls? I'm done. Done with women, done trying.*

I learned in college that isolation is easier, and that's the route I took. I withdrew from healthy friendships rather than risk the contempt of other women. It wasn't that I didn't *want* friendship; it just hurt too much to try.

Community is hard. It looks great on paper, doesn't it? It looks fabulous on Instagram when we see images of #squadgoals and established friend groups. But we forget that those friend groups weren't always together. Community takes time, effort, and—worst of all—risk. Being friends with other women exposes us to potential hurt, and as we go deeper and our most vulnerable parts are brought to light, shame. Isolation is so much easier!

I was extremely sensitive to mean girls in college because high school was fresh in my mind. Even though I was homeschooled, there was a hierarchy of "cool" just like any other system of young people—and as I mentioned before, I wasn't in it. Constantly being left out or treated as ignorant made me defensive and withdrawn. *I don't like women,* I decided.

I'd love to say my view of other women didn't negatively affect the rest of my life, but the opposite was true. I became critical and judgmental of other girls. I viewed them as a threat—a threat to my emotional safety, my identity, and my collection of guy friends. My bitterness and skepticism were thinly veiled, and I attracted girls just like me. Toxic friendships became my pattern. In a twist of irony, the person hurt by weak, immature women became in turn weak and immature. I became the very woman I despised the most: a mean girl.

Right before I got married, my best friend "broke up" with me and dropped out of my wedding. It was a crushing blow. Still reeling from what happened, I joined a women's Bible study at the church Josh and I started attending. Walking into a roomful of unfamiliar faces brought my insecurity to the surface, trembling under my skin. I waited for a snide comment or a contemptuous look I was trained to expect. But it didn't come. The women—older women, women with kids, young women—embraced me as if I'd always been one of them. They made me feel known. And not just known, but *wanted.*

Looking back, I see how being in true, godly community takes the stinger out of the mean girl. Mean women don't last long in a place of genuine vulnerability. The unfamiliarity of being among people who actually care, who expect you to share your struggles and insecurities, will either send you running to your comfort zone or bring you freedom. The latter was true for me.

That first study time was the beginning of my healing. I'd been hurt by Christian women—and it was Christian women God used to heal me. In the ensuing years, it was women in that small church and the one after it, when we moved to Pennsylvania, who helped to heal years of fearful resentment I harbored toward community. I learned to stop viewing other women as potential threats or enemies but instead saw them as future friends. I learned that God's heart, from the beginning to the end of time, was for His people to be in community.

Here in northern Michigan we have lakes in every direction. By January, many of our inland lakes are frozen over, and by March, our Lake Michigan bay freezes over as well. People love to skate and snowmobile on the ice, but to do so, you have to take a risk of falling in. Even during the coldest winter, stepping onto the ice is dangerous. But oh, how beautiful it is when you take the chance! There is nothing like wind whipping through your hair as you spin on a frozen lake or fly across it at top speed.

Cultivating relationships often feels like stepping onto that ice. You're risking a chilly dunk in failed friendship. There's a chance of being left in the cold. You may jeopardize your own emotional safety. But God has shown us that relationship is worth it—not just by putting two people in the garden instead of one, but in pursuing relationship with us Himself. Think about it: The God who was entirely sufficient in and of Himself chose to create people for the sake of relationship. He called Israel to social justice, to honor God through their relationships. And Jesus came to provide a perfect relationship between us and God. Relationship is not optional! God Himself embraced the risk, and we're called to do the same.

So what keeps us from these relationships God wants for our souls? I see a few patterns.

- Fear: We fear what others think of us, and ultimately we fear man more than we revere God and His heart for our lives. We're so terrified of rejection by *people* we forget we are accepted by God. We let fear, not love, dictate our relationships.

- Insecurity: Fear and insecurity go hand in hand. We aren't secure in our place in the world, our purpose, or our identities so we feel threatened by the people around us. Relationship exposes insecurity so we avoid community to avoid being vulnerable.

- Pride: We don't want to be accountable. We don't want people to know our deepest secrets and struggles, even though exposing them would bring freedom. We would rather live in bondage than let our façade be stripped away.

When fear, insecurity, and pride motivate us, our relationships can't beat to the rhythm of God's heart. If we say we follow Jesus, if we truly want to go deeper with Him and grow up into women of God, we have to acknowledge where we're letting fear, insecurity, and pride determine how our relationships go. We *can* have positive relationships with people, including other women. And the Bible shows us how.

GOD'S HEART FOR OUR RELATIONSHIPS

I receive a lot of questions each week from my readers, but one in particular has shown up multiple times: "How do I find contentment as a single person?" I believe contentment, particularly regarding relationships, is harder to attain than ever before. This isn't just because we live in a media-saturated society where romance is pushed on us from every angle. We lack contentment in singleness because we are painfully *isolated*.

Facebook, Instagram, Snapchat, Marco Polo, texting, email—we are connected in a million different ways. But for many, these connections are surface-level. Lacking the intimate knowledge of Christian community, single people become consumed with finding "the one." Their desire for a dating relationship is aggravated because they are missing some of the deep, satisfying relationships God intends for them.

I think we've all been at a wedding where, during a sand-pouring or candle-lighting or knot-tying, someone reads Ecclesiastes 4:9-10: "Two are better than one, because they have a good return for their labor. If either of them falls down, one can help the other up. But pity anyone who falls and has no one to help them up." We've assigned this verse to romantic relationships. But context indicates it's more likely referring to *community at large*. Two are indeed better than one. Even better than two? A gathering of believers supporting one another in their walk with God! God's plan for His people is for men and women to live at peace with one another, doing right by one another, spreading the gospel side by side. When we exalt marriage as the ideal, we miss God's ultimate mark. Rather than encouraging people to strive for one relationship as "fulfillment," we should encourage a community of fulfilling relationships.

That's how isolation can be overcome. Godly community fulfills us in a way even marriage fails to do at times (and acts as support when marriages struggle). We need fellow Christ-followers. It's that simple. Isolation might seem like an easy way to avoid conflict or pain, but it is one of the most foolish decisions we can make. Proverbs 18:1 says, "Whoever isolates himself seeks his own desire; he breaks out against all sound judgment" (ESV). Isolating ourselves is the opposite of good decision making. Why? Because of the impact it has on our character.

Proverbs 27:17 gives us a visual for how relationships shape and mold us: "As iron sharpens iron, so one person sharpens another." Have you ever watched a blacksmith do his work? Seen how he heats the metal to white-hot before pounding with his metal hammer? Sparks fly every direction. But when he's done, you can see that the heat and pounding crafted that metal into a thing of beauty. You can't work with metal without using another metal to shape and sharpen the object you are wanting to mold.

Such is the case with godly friendships. Yes, being in relationship opens us up to the pain of pounding. But a loving friend will not rebuke unnecessarily; the sharpening is a vital part of our growth. Their intimate knowledge of our heart, our soul, and our dream uniquely prepares them to refine us, to encourage us, and to help us grow into women of deep faith. God uses Christian community to do much of His intended work in our hearts and character.

IMPERFECT PEOPLE, PERFECT UNITY

It takes heat and pressure to refine metal. It takes heat and pressure to refine relationships—which means relationships, especially among Christians, don't always go as we hope. Church hurt is real.

For many years I was either too young or too removed to see the problems in my church communities. All I saw were smiles, hugs, handshakes, potlucks—if there was conflict, I didn't know. But as Josh and I started to take a more active role in our community, we realized just how much human drama exists in the church. It both surprised and saddened us (and gave us a deep appreciation for our friends in ministry!). After a particularly hard season of conflict among Christians, we looked at each other in bewilderment. "The Bible talks about unity," I told Josh. "But I have no idea how to accomplish that in this situation."

To be honest, unity isn't what I wanted. I wanted justice. I wanted the problem people to go away. I wanted (and often still want) the conflict-causers to stop instigating dissension and find a new community to disrupt. But this isn't what God asks of me...of us. Jesus told us to love our enemies, even when those enemies look like other Christians. Perhaps I should say especially when those enemies look like other Christians. This is one of the hardest parts of going deeper with God.

Division in the body of Christ is the opposite of what God wants, and it's exactly what the Enemy works to achieve. A "house divided against itself will not stand" (Matthew 12:22-28 NKJV), Jesus said; we can't stand together as a community if we are at each other's throats.

The struggle for unity is nothing new in the church. The New Testament is full of exhortations to walk in step with our fellow believers. Here are just a few:

> Above all, keep loving one another earnestly, since love covers a multitude of sins. Show hospitality to one another without grumbling. As each has received a gift, use it to serve one another, as good stewards of God's varied grace (1 Peter 4:8-10 ESV).

> Let us consider how to stir up one another to love and good works, not neglecting to meet together, as is the habit of some, but encouraging one another, and all the more as you see the Day drawing near (Hebrews 10:24-25 ESV).

> Love one another with brotherly affection. Outdo one another in showing honor (Romans 12:10 ESV).

How do imperfect people achieve unity? The answer is simple, but incredibly hard: by loving one another. You can't love someone and condemn them at the same time! But man, is this hard—especially when you're a truth-speaker like me. Yet this is God's expectation. Just as He graciously bears with us each day—with our unfaithfulness, our sins, our begrudging discipleship—we're expected to bear with others. When I think of the word *bear*, I picture a person carrying a burden. When we bear with others, we're taking up the emotional load of that relationship. We're laying down our lives (John 15:12-15)…just as Jesus did for us.

Last week I was feeling very worn down, tired of bearing with a situation where repeated sin patterns were wounding me and many others. I stopped by the coffee shop where my sister works and laid it on the table. "I want it to be over," I told her. She handed me my coffee and said, "I guess God probably wants our sin to be over too." Whoa. Reality check! Our sin grieves God even more than the sin of our fellow believers grieves us, and yet He promises, "If [you] confess [your] sins, [I am] faithful and just and will forgive" them (1 John 1:9). *Forgiveness* is a hard word. But it's a lot easier to give grace when you remember how much grace you've been given.

In John 15:12-15, Jesus said,

> This is my commandment, that you love one another as I have loved you. Greater love has no one than this, that someone lay down his life for his friends. You are my friends if you do what I command you. No longer do I call you servants, for the servant does not know what his master is doing; but I have called you friends, for all that I have heard from my Father I have made known to you (ESV).

The deeper we go in faith, the closer we draw to the heart of God and the more our lives should emulate His patient love for the sinful.

That's hard for me to write; I feel the conviction in my own heart this very moment. But this is His commandment: Love others as He has loved us. Patiently. Truthfully. Gently. Consistently. Willingly. It's a supernatural call, so good thing we have a supernatural Spirit. We never could love others this way on our own imperfect strength. Leaning into God's love for us is what spurs us on to love for others. This love, in turn, results in unity.

Our church hurts are healed by God's love for us. God's love for us enables love for others. Our love for others points them to the love of God. On and on the circle goes, drawing everyone closer to the Christian community God intended from the dawn of time.

LOVE AND BOUNDARIES

Developing community, growing in unity—these things take time. They also take effort. Our efforts to love aren't limited to serving, however. The grace we give sometimes requires laying down boundaries. Jesus called us to love, but love is not the absence of boundaries. Jesus Himself gently and firmly stood up to manipulative people—not to prove He was right, but to express God's truths. Sometimes the most loving thing you can do is set a firm boundary.

Boundaries are a necessary part of loving others in a fallen world, especially when God has given us work, husbands, and families to steward. Sacrificing His greatest gifts to preserve a toxic relationship, to avoid conflict? How backward! God works in the lives of difficult people—but He doesn't always need us in order to do so. One of the most freeing things we can realize is that we are not Jesus. We are no one's personal savior. But by the Spirit's leading, we can be patient, kind, not envious, not boastful, humble, honorable to others—all 1 Corinthians 13 attributes of love—and still walk by wisdom in our relationships. This call to love and community is not a call to abandon wisdom. Sometimes love itself is a boundary, because love always speaks God's truth.

Many Christians struggle to know when a boundary is healthy and when it's a lack of grace. God has shown us grace, after all. Aren't we supposed to show grace to others? While we're absolutely called to be patient with the shortcomings of our fellow believers, sin still has consequences. When a believer shows repeated patterns of sin that wound others and divide community, he or she should be confronted (Matthew 18:15-17 outlines how to go about this). If that person refuses to listen and change, a boundary is the next step.

When you get to this point in a relationship, it's very easy to let bitterness reign. I'm personally thinking of a situation that has brought me to my knees in desperate prayer. Division and conflict just don't seem to stop even after boundaries have been placed. But as I pray about this situation, I clearly see God's intent. No matter what choices sinful people make, God's goal is restoration. That should be my goal too.

God's restoration of all things is the hope of the gospel (Revelation 21:1-5). The struggles of earthly community will be but a blip on the screen when we experience the complete unity of heaven. This eternal perspective helps us bear with difficult brothers and sisters, put down roots in community, and pursue relationships even when they pose a risk.

TO LOVE IS TO BE VULNERABLE

Earlier this week I visited a friend's house. As my three-year-old played with colored pencils on the floor, we talked about God's leading on my friend's life and the direction she felt Him calling her to go. From an outside perspective, I could see how the last year had shaped her and was more and more excited as she shared this new season. "This is amazing!" I told her. "I think God is on the brink of doing something exciting in this job." She laughed. "This is why we need to be in godly community, I guess—I was having a hard time seeing that!"

My friend was right: Godly community grants us support and perspective. It checks our choices and motives. As we walk closer with God, we walk closer with His other children. This is perhaps the most beautiful part of all, because it gives us a little taste of heaven long before we get there.

Community is a journey. As we grow in Jesus, we learn how to strike the delicate balance of loving others and not being bound to their approval or toxicity. Perhaps you're reading this and wondering, *But how?* The truth? I can't answer that for your specific situation. All I can do is point you to a deeper, daily walk with Jesus. Because when you're walking closely with Jesus, daily opening His Word, becoming a learner, a disciple, your heart is tuned to hear the Spirit speak. Even if I were to tell you exactly what to do in all your relationships, it would defeat the purpose of this book: to point you to the overcoming power of Jesus Christ and the freedom of a daily walk with Him. Checklists are not the solution to fallen relationships; a closer walk with Jesus is!

A deep, vibrant Christian life overcomes isolation. But realizing God's heart for community didn't remove all relational conflict from my life, and it won't for you either. Friendships wax and wane over the years, we will be hurt, and we will hurt others. But we can see these situations with eternal perspective.

Christian community, in a fallen world, will always take work—but it's the best work we can do. We cannot flatter ourselves into thinking we can do this life alone. We need men and women around us who are serious about following Jesus. Relationship is a risk, but

it's a risk modeled by Jesus and required by the Lord. C.S. Lewis put
it best when he said:

> To love at all is to be vulnerable. Love anything, and your
> heart will certainly be wrung and possibly be broken. If
> you want to make sure of keeping it intact, you must
> give your heart to no one, not even to an animal. Wrap it
> carefully round with hobbies and little luxuries; avoid all
> entanglements; lock it up safe in the casket or coffin of
> your selfishness. But in that casket—safe, dark, motion-
> less, airless—it will change. It will not be broken; it will
> become unbreakable, impenetrable, irredeemable.[1]

Love, by nature, requires vulnerability. Loving God and others opens us up to a world of hurt—but it also opens us up to a
life that matters. One day our hurts will be healed finally, eternally.
Would you live avoiding the hurt, living in an ivory tower of isolation, if it meant avoiding the very life God had for you? Abundance
with Jesus requires stepping out into risky waters—including the
risky waters of relationships. We can't always trust people, but we
can always trust *Him*. He is our confidence and our healing, and
He empowers us to have relationships that defy everything we've
known before.

WHAT YOU CAN DO TODAY

1. Think about your friendships and write down some thoughts. How would you characterize the relationships you have? Are they deep, shallow, strong, weak, familiar? Are you content with where they are, or do you wish they would change?

2. Consider your perspective on vulnerability. Do you hold back from giving yourself to relationships because you've been hurt before? What would have happened to us if Jesus had lived this way?

3. What do you think about the balance of love and boundaries? Consider what boundaries you may need to set in your relationships so you can give your best to them.

10

AN AUDIENCE OF ONE: CONQUERING FEAR OF MAN

He was about to break up with me. I could just tell.

Sitting on the edge of my dorm room bunk, I swung my leg like a pendulum: back and forth, back and forth. Back and forth like this relationship. I could feel him pulling away and I was mad about it; mad, because rejection was the one thing I hated most.

I don't even remember how I ended it, but I did. I ended it before he could end it with me. I wasn't about to let myself get wounded by yet another guy; I was not going to be his fool. Much like I did with my female friendships, I got out before it got too hard.

It's funny when I look back to see how intensely I hated rejection—or even the *potential* for rejection. Though I never said it in so many words, I truly believed that being the one who did the rejecting meant I was in control. I could protect my heart, protect my vulnerability. But when you hate something that much, it reveals a hard truth: The thing you hate controls you.

It wasn't the rejection itself that controlled me, but something deeper. Something we battle on a daily basis in the form of anger, discontent, and bitterness. What controlled me and controls many people today is as old as humanity itself. The King James Bible called it "fear of man" (Proverbs 29:25).

In one of life's great dichotomies, we fear losing what we value most—even when the thing we value is destroying us. We desperately want to be accepted by people. We want to be popular with women and men, to be celebrated and honored and adored. In my own life, people pulling away meant the loss of everything I held dear. If I could hear the hurt coming like a freight train, before it could hit me, I threw the tracks. Better a relationship crash and burn than run me over.

We're often oblivious to how this fear controls us; fear of man is hard to recognize. We can deceive ourselves into thinking it's love: serving others dutifully, sacrificially, then seething as lack of appreciation sparks bitterness in our hearts. Or we bend over backward for our friends, our spouse, or a family member out of "love," only to become enraged when their responses aren't what we hoped. We blame the other person for how we feel, but deep down the issue is in our own hearts. We desperately want people to approve, accept, and admire us, and we're angry when they don't.

Rejection is one of the most uncontrollable feelings we face. We naturally want to protect ourselves from it. Anger, bitterness, grudges—these *feel* like control. In a twist of irony, we think we can control a situation by holding on to what happened, when really we are the ones being controlled. If we can't live our lives free from people and their offenses, who is actually losing? In my own experience, the offender usually carries on as if nothing ever happened. The one who holds on to the hurt is the one who suffers.

ANGER, BITTERNESS, GRUDGES—THESE *FEEL* LIKE CONTROL...THE ONE WHO HOLDS ON TO THE HURT IS THE ONE WHO SUFFERS.

WREAKING MY OWN JUSTICE

I try to be quick at forgiving those who offend me. It's when they offend *others* that I lose my cool. Hurt me? I want to seek peace. Hurt my family? *Just you wait.* Fierce loyalty and defensiveness bubble to the surface, and it takes everything I have not to go into full-on attack mode. Sometimes I still do—and not just with friends and family. Like the time I faced down a businessman in an airport for screaming at the attendant (I think yelling at *him* for yelling at *her* was more than a little hypocritical). My bitterness stems from what is initially a healthy desire. Loyalty, justice for the underdog? These are good things to want. Where I go wrong—where everyone goes wrong—is when I believe justice is all up to me.

Paul quoted the Lord in Romans 12:19, saying, "Do not take revenge, my dear friends, but leave room for God's wrath, for it is written: 'It is mine to avenge; I will repay,' says the Lord." Vengeance—the wreaking of justice—is not for human hands to bring about. Our imperfection makes us unqualified to act as final judge, but when we see injustice, we want to do something. So we hold grudges. We withhold kindness. We slander and gossip. We'd never wreak actual revenge, not in a *Count of Monte Cristo* kind of way. But we do it passively through our words, thoughts, and attitudes. Deep down we don't believe that God will work justice for the offended and hurt, so we take matters into our own hands…and allow bitterness into our hearts.

Now, to clarify: Just because God is the arbiter of justice doesn't mean we stand by in silence when people are abused. We are called to advocate for the hurting, speak up for the voiceless, and walk with those less privileged than ourselves. There is a biblical way to address sin and injustice, and it involves directly confronting the people involved. Fear of man doesn't allow for biblical confrontation, because the utmost concern is control, not reconciliation.

In the previous chapter I mentioned my best friendship that fell apart right before my wedding. As the relationship grew strained, I frantically tried to figure out what went wrong. I reached out to ask why. My friend was honest with me: I was negative and argumentative, and our relationship wasn't something she wanted to pursue anymore. I was crushed…and then I was angry. *Does she really think she had no part in this?* I seethed. *Does she accept no responsibility for her role in this story?*

I wish I could say I let it go after a few weeks, but bitterness over that friendship followed me for years. For most of that time I was angry because of how I thought she had handled herself in our friendship. I felt very justified in my anger and rehearsed my reasoning to Josh many times. Two years, a move, and a baby later, that breakup *still* had a hold on me. I remember sitting in my duplex living room with my four-month-old daughter, sifting through an old email inbox. My friend's name popped on the screen, and I felt… sadness. Tears welled in my eyes as I thought of all we had lost. I missed her. Deep down, I wasn't angry. I was heartbroken.

What I thought was a best friendship was really my idolizing a friend's approval. When I'd first reached out for reconciliation, what I really craved was control. She was slipping away, the friend into whom I'd poured so much of my life, so I tried to control my way back in. When she ended it anyway, I tried to control my emotions through anger. When anger didn't satisfy, I tried to control the loss by endlessly processing our breakup in my mind. Because I didn't process my emotions in a godly way, and because I was more concerned about the opinions of *one person* than the opinion of God, the cycle of fear, rejection, and control entrapped me on every side. What I didn't know then, I see now: I feared the loss of human approval more than I trusted God to satisfy my heart.

This is the door through which bitterness walks. It's the place

I FEARED THE
LOSS OF HUMAN
APPROVAL MORE
THAN I TRUSTED
GOD TO SATISFY
MY HEART.

entitlement makes a home. Fear of rejection is just a means to the Enemy's end: to keep our eyes off Christ and on ourselves. Or, if he can't keep our eyes on ourselves, to keep them fixed on the lives of others.

FEAR OF MAN IS A TRAP

Proverbs 29:25 says, "The fear of man lays a snare, but whoever trusts in the LORD is safe" (ESV). A snare is a trap. I have a friend who is a trapper, mainly for coyotes (a nuisance here in Michigan). I asked him what the trapping process looks like. "A trapper looks for signs, geographical features, and food sources to know where to set traps for animals," he said. "To camouflage the trap, some traps are buried lightly in sand or leaves, and others are camouflaged with sticks or branches."

The trapper isn't setting his trap just anywhere, hoping for an animal to happen across it. He is intentional with where and how he sets the snare, using materials that look both appealing and safe. He sets it where the animal has frequently gone before. And since a trapper isn't using force to capture the animal, he has to use *deceit*. For the animal, what looks like the same, normal route is no longer safe. It might *look* like the right path, but it's a path that leads to death.

Proverbs 29:25 doesn't say that the fear of man *is* a snare. Fear of man *lays* a snare. Fear of man is not the trap, but the trapper. When we allow our desire for man's approval to control our decisions, our whole lives are open to the deceit of the Enemy. Further, as we repeatedly walk the path of fear, the Enemy knows just where and how to lay his snare. He camouflages his work to make it seem safe and uses the same pitfalls over and over because we're still walking the same path. Until we get our eyes off of man and onto Jesus, we'll always find ourselves bound to man's changing desires.

The opinions of people do change—a lot. They change with the seasons and the trends, and they differ from person to person. I know this from my own experience. Recovering people pleaser that I am, I went through a season of deep insecurity around other women. One of my biggest hang-ups was how I appeared to others.

Where I live in the rural Midwest, "dressed up" is defined as "not wearing jeans." I've always enjoyed looking nice, and usually do my hair and makeup each morning. I'm also an avid bargain shopper and love putting together dressy outfits for the average day. This personal love of the chic lifestyle couldn't be reconciled with my fear of man. I was terrified I'd come off as high maintenance to those around me. Or that I'd make someone feel bad for wearing jeans. Or that they'd assume I was snobby because I always wore heels.

Every person has different preferences. So rather than be who I really was, I changed myself. I'd buy a red university hoodie…and wear it only around people who loved hoodies. New friends coming to dinner? I'd dress far more casually than I was comfortable with, just in case they would feel judged by my attire.

At the time I thought I was being sensitive and loving. But I was miserable. I began to resent people for "making me" work so hard for their approval…when they never asked me to change myself! I held others accountable for a law I created. I lived for man's approval, but I decided what needed to be approved. That's enough to make a person crazy, and that's exactly what it did to me. I was ensnared by my own fear of man's opinion, and consequently trapped in bitterness, anger, and judgment. Through time with God in His Word and prayer, He showed me how I was using my outward appearance to worship the approval of others. As I laid this idol down, I was free: Free to dress how I like to dress. Free to be the person I am. Free to love others without worrying about their perception of me.

God knows what happens when we fix our eyes on man, which

is why He warns against it all throughout Scripture. One person who had every reason to seek man's approval was the apostle Paul. Paul was successful in every area of his field and far exceeded other teachers in qualification (2 Corinthians 11:21-29). But none of this had value to him. Later, in his letter to the Galatian church, Paul affirmed what is most important: fear of God.

> Am I now trying to win the approval of human beings, or of God? Or am I trying to please people? If I were still trying to please people, I would not be a servant of Christ (Galatians 1:10).

If I were still trying to please people. I love that Paul admitted he was once a people pleaser—bold, confident, fearless Paul! But Paul also shows us that pleasing people and serving Christ are at two ends of the life spectrum. You can't do both, and you certainly can't do both at the same time. When counseling Timothy, the young pastor of the church at Ephesus, Paul told him, "God gave us a spirit not of fear but of power and love and self-control" (2 Timothy 1:7 ESV). Some translations say "sound mind" instead of self-control. A spirit of fear results in weakness, fakeness, and confusion. God's Spirit leads us to a life of strength, kindness, and wisdom.

BOWED DOWN AND BURDENED

There was another man in Scripture who had a lot to say about the fear of man. Isaiah was a prophet given a painful life calling: to preach God's message to people who didn't want to hear it. Isaiah spent most of his life warning the people of Israel about the coming consequences of their idolatry. I imagine the people weren't fans of Isaiah, with his constant talk of judgment. But Isaiah feared God more than the opinions of people, and his prophetic words are still with us today.

In Isaiah 51, God spoke through Isaiah to the people of Israel, addressing their fear of man. The whole passage is a beautiful depiction of God's power and grace, but here's the convicting part:

> I, I am he who comforts you;
> > who are you that you are afraid of man who dies,
> > of the son of man who is made like grass,
> and have forgotten the LORD, your Maker,
> > who stretched out the heavens
> > and laid the foundations of the earth,
> and you fear continually all the day
> > because of the wrath of the oppressor,
> when he sets himself to destroy?
> > And where is the wrath of the oppressor?
> He who is bowed down shall speedily be released;
> > he shall not die and go down to the pit,
> > neither shall his bread be lacking (verses 12-14 ESV).

I'm overwhelmed by the beauty of this passage. God—Creator, King, Lord of creation—promises to release those who are bowed down. Picture a person beneath a heavy burden, one she can barely carry. As she struggles down the path of life with her heavy load, Jesus comes alongside her, lifts the burden off her shoulders, and takes it onto His. That's what He does for us! And not only that— He remains with us for the duration of the journey (John 15).

God promises to release us. And not just release us, but to do so quickly. This begs the question, *How did we get burdened in the first place?* Go back up to verses 12 and 13 in Isaiah 51: "Who are you that you are afraid of man who dies, of the son of man who is made like grass, and have forgotten the LORD, your Maker?" (ESV). Israel was bowed down under the weight of their own fear. Like Israel, we know we can never please people. We know it's unhealthy to live for their approval. And yet over and over again we go to the altar, sacrificing our time, our marriages, our families, and our God-given gifts in worship of human admiration.

Fear of man is a burden. It's a burden that makes us forget who God is, what He has done, and what He promises to do in the future. But Isaiah 51 doesn't leave us facedown to the ground, crushed by the weight of man's approval (or lack thereof). It points us to the hope we have in Jesus Christ, who "bore our sins in His body on the cross, so that we might die to sin and live to righteousness" (1 Peter 2:24 NASB). And what no one wants to say, but what needs to be said: Fear of man is a sin. It's a sin because it shifts our worship away from God and fixes our hearts on a god who cannot save. Thank the Lord for the overcoming power of Jesus! We don't have to live under the weight of fear. We don't have to live bound to old sins and patterns of behavior. We can speedily be released.

WALKING FREE

Being released from fear isn't beyond the grasp of the average believer. It's for the lowliest among us, those who need His freedom most. It's for women who've tried to please people and instead found themselves rejected by them. It's for women who put their identity in their relationships with others instead of in their relationship with Christ. It's for women who are searching for meaning and purpose—purpose that lasts beyond the opinions of mother, sister, and friend. Jesus's freedom is for women who keep coming to the well of human opinion and pulling up empty buckets.

Speaking of empty buckets, if anyone in the Bible had reason to fear people, I think the Samaritan woman wins. Her reputation was in the gutter. And given the times in which she lived, she didn't just have the opinions of man to fear, but a real fear of men in general. I am reading into the text a little here, but I imagine—if the Samaritan woman was several times divorced or abandoned—she was not a big fan of the opposite sex. Hurt had replaced hopes. Trust had turned to fear. And the crazy thing about deeply rooted fear is how it manifests as confidence. The Samaritan woman interacted with Jesus even though she knew it was not culturally appropriate. She *knew* she wasn't supposed to talk to Him, but she joined the conversation—cold, defensive, pragmatic. Her attitude was almost, *Whatever, let's talk about this "living water."*

Few people in Scripture experienced as much rejection as the Samaritan woman, yet even fewer people allowed that rejection to become a testimony of faith. And this woman wasn't just excluded from the cool kids' club; she was rejected on many levels: by Israel for being a half-breed, by men (possibly for being barren), and perhaps by her own people for being unable to "keep" a husband. How can you experience that much rejection and not be bitter? Yet in the short glimpse we get of her in John 4, a transformation occurs. Jesus met her in the middle of her loneliness, at a point where man's approval wasn't even possible. There, where fear of man accomplished nothing, Jesus accomplished everything. She was bowed down beneath the rejection of others. Jesus released her. Her faith made her whole.

> Then, leaving her water jar, the woman went back to the town and said to the people, "Come, see a man who told me everything I ever did. Could this be the Messiah?" (verses 28-29).

Released from fear, rejection, and bitterness, she *ran* to the people of the city, unashamed to advertise her past. Fear of man had no hold on her. She didn't care what people thought! She just wanted them to meet Jesus. And they did.

The Samaritan woman believed Jesus's words *more* than the condemnation around her, and it broke her yoke of shame. She is an example of what life can look like when we don't just believe in Jesus, but actually believe Him. Actually believe what He says about who we are and to whom we answer. Jesus frees us from fear of man, but we have to embrace His freedom. We have a part in our own freedom story: to daily choose His unshifting approval or to live captive to fear and bitterness.

The choice looks simple on paper, but it's a step of faith. It's putting so much faith in who Jesus is and what He did on the cross, you're willing to stop measuring yourself by what others think. For most of us, that's a big step. No more comparing? No more controlling? No more being controlled? It sounds amazing, but walking it out is unfamiliar territory. We act like the proverbial bird in the cage, who, when offered freedom, flies right back inside because it's familiar and safe. We'd rather stay safe and caged than risk the beauty of an open sky. But Jesus did not die so we could live in a cage of fear. He came to give us life, abundantly: a life of eternal merit.

How do we actually grasp this abundance? How do we live emotionally, spiritually, free from the fear of man and all that it entails? It starts with our reverence for God. Our minds and hearts can't be full of fear and love at the same time, because perfect love casts out fear (1 John 4:18). God's love for us, our love for Him…these cultivate an environment where fear cannot grow. It's too bright with the light of grace. Reverence for God is recognizing that He is beyond us, yet also with us, striving for us because He loves us. When you know and believe the love God has for you, victory over fear becomes a lifestyle.

First John 2 says, "God's word remains in you, and you have had victory over the evil one" (verse 14 HCSB). The Word of God is what the Spirit uses to help you walk in victory, declaring truth to you in the time of need. The truth of God abides, rests, and takes up residence in you when you intentionally invest time in the Word. This truth is the lens through which we view all worldviews, perspectives, and opinions. God is our first stop.

But what's even more encouraging? We have *already* had victory! John wrote in past tense because Jesus overcame sin and fear on our behalf. Fear is finished. Any time we give in to it, we're shifting our eyes off Jesus's victory and elevating the opinions of people above the opinions of God. We're shackling ourselves to the prison of approval, when all Jesus wants is to set us free.

WHAT YOU CAN DO TODAY

1. Write out the people whose opinions you fear the most. Take a moment to commit those people to the grace and power of God.

2. Release your burdens to the Lord right now. I recommend writing them out—every sense of rejection, inadequacy, and fear that comes to your mind at this moment. Then reread Isaiah 51:11-14 and praise God for His acceptance, grace, and strength.

3. After today, be mindful of your motives. Before you take an action, ask yourself, "Am I doing this because I fear what someone will think of me? Would I still do this if I knew for a fact I didn't need to in order to be the woman God desires me to be?"

11

EVERYTHING I EVER DID: OVERCOMING SHAME

M y fingers trembled on the keyboard. I stopped typing my blog post and buried my face in my hands.

What will they think of me?

The cursor blinked at me, and I blinked back through tears. I knew who would read it: my closest family, my friends from high school, my college dorm mates, my former coworkers from ten different jobs. They would read it and know everything I'd hidden in those double-minded years. *God, help me. Help me show what You've done for me, even when it exposes everything I've ever done.*

Sharing my testimony of sexual sin, shame, and God's redemption was one of the most terrifying moments of my life. I knew it would expose things I'd never planned to bring to the light. Though I struggled against my fear of man's opinion, an unexplainable confidence filled my heart. My story *had* to be shared. The story was more important than what people would think. And after years of keeping silent because of shame, my faith in God's redemption was finally greater.

Brené Brown, a leading secular writer on the topic of shame, says shame is "the experience or fear of believing we're not worthy of connection."[1] Shame prevents vulnerability, because vulnerability puts us at emotional risk. As Christians, our innate knowledge of what is good and what is evil makes us far more conscious of shame when it comes. And even though Romans 8:1 promises, "There is now no condemnation for those who are in Christ Jesus," many Christians live in bondage to the things they've done, the thoughts they've embraced, and the people they used to be.

How desperately I wanted to be "cool" when I felt the most shame. In those years of bondage to sexual sin, I developed a hardened exterior to control how I was perceived. My own heart condemned me; I couldn't bear the condemnation of others too. It was easier to act confident than to do the heart work necessary for true inner confidence. That's why my bravado had such a biting edge—and why my relationships suffered. My bondage to shame was a driving factor behind my insecurity, legalism, and fear of man.

Shame makes us do strange things. It makes us act in ways inconsistent with what we know is true. In my own battle with shame, I'd elevate what I'd done above God's character until my past seemed too dark for redemption. Shame was my greatest fear, so I put on the best "good girl" act I knew. I covered up my insecurity with confidence and tried to shame others before they shamed me. When we live by shame, we live in a state of self-protection. We're never real or vulnerable.

Our culture recognizes the negative effects of shame. But the secular solution to shame falls sadly short. The world's promise: Change how we view ourselves, change the culture, change the world one by one, and shame will be defeated. Embrace "your truth" and nothing will undermine your confidence. The non-Christian reference point for overcoming shame is *within ourselves*. But what if our *selves* are the problem in the first place?

TRUE CONFIDENCE
CANNOT COME FROM SELF

If we view ourselves as unworthy, we will act unworthy. The world knows this to be true, so it approaches shame from a self-centered perspective. "If you love yourself," the books and magazines and entrepreneurs tell us, "it won't matter what you've done. You're worthy *just because you're you*." This mantra—spoken, written, shared on social media—sounds so good. But how many of us know in the core of our being that what we've done really is a big deal? How many of us realize that saying we're worthy, no matter how many times, can't actually change how we see ourselves?

Shame comes from something we believe within ourselves, so searching within ourselves for answers doesn't make sense. We can't be completely free from the shame of what we've done by learning more about who we are. Even if we get to a positive view of self by sheer willpower, what about when we mess up? How do we view ourselves when we've blown it? How do we recover from that? There's no redemption for big mistakes in the secular approach to shame and brokenness. There's just hoping it goes away with time. And some things aren't healed by the passage of years; some brokenness isn't put back together with "I'm sorry." There's a side of shame that's beyond our control, a side that self-actualization can't even begin to fix.

When I typed up the blog post sharing my testimony of sexual addiction, shame talked into my ear the entire time. Telling myself, "I'm worthy because of who I am!" never would have given

WE CAN'T BE
COMPLETELY FREE
FROM THE SHAME OF
WHAT WE'VE DONE
BY LEARNING MORE
ABOUT WHO WE ARE.

me the confidence to hit *publish*. The things I'd done made me completely *un*worthy. No one could argue otherwise. Loving myself more didn't change the damage I'd done to myself or to others. So I shared my testimony not because I loved myself but because I finally accepted God's love *for me*. His was a love I never could deserve, a grace I could finally experience. I wasn't ignoring the existence of my sin, hoping it would go away. My sin—my shame—was completely eradicated in Christ. This was the basis for my confidence.

When we allow our brokenness and shame to loom larger than Christ's sacrifice, we're submitting to an ungodly authority. The past is not our god. Jesus, who resurrected from the dead to overcome sin and the grave—*He* is our God! Only when we keep this perspective do we view ourselves in the correct light…the light of freedom.

FACING OUR BROKENNESS

Our brokenness has marketable value in today's society. It's our brokenness that self-help entrepreneurs want to repair. It's brokenness that many women's ministries welcome, which is great, but once the brokenness has been welcomed, what happens with it? Is it healed? Is it replaced? Is it redeemed? Too often, none of these things are true for the broken people seeking help. Their brokenness is rehashed and embraced and celebrated as normal, but true freedom—the kind where your brokenness is made whole and you live unshackled from your past—doesn't exist. Sure, Jesus redeems us. But it's an eternal redemption, not a present one. This is why thousands of women exist both in Christ *and* in shame. Thousands are self-helping their way through life, reading the same book—just a different author—longing to be told they're beautiful, but never really believing God can change the parts of them that they know need to be redeemed.

THOUSANDS ARE
SELF-HELPING THEIR
WAY THROUGH
LIFE...NEVER REALLY
BELIEVING GOD
FOR CHANGE.

For those in Christ, something better *does* exist. It's something better than gathering up the shards of our lives, pulling ourselves up by the bootstraps, and trudging through each day by a Bible verse and willpower. It's the "something better" Jesus offered the woman at the well, the "something better" of John 10:10. And it starts by facing everything we've ever done.

Facing the reality of sin and shame is one of the hardest things we do. Adam and Eve weren't willing to do that. Thousands of years later, neither are we. We're still here stitching fig leaves together, hoping the façade we design will shield us from exposure. But nothing we craft can ever fully cover us, can it? Our attempts at covering brokenness—hiding it from the light of God's redemption—cause it to stay with us for weeks, months, and years. Brokenness becomes part of us. And once it's part of us, we don't see the problem with the temporal hope of the self-help gospel. Complete redemption and healing isn't even on our radar; we're just looking for more fig leaves!

The Bible is very clear: Jesus did not die so we could identify as broken. He died so we could be reconciled to a holy God. He died to secure us an eternal home. The rippling effect of Jesus's sacrifice influences every aspect of our daily lives. In Romans 8, the apostle Paul broke down all the times in life when Jesus overcomes on our behalf. It's quite the list:

> Who shall separate us from the love of Christ? Shall trouble or hardship or persecution or famine or nakedness or danger or sword? As it is written:
>
> > "For your sake we face death all day long;
> > we are considered as sheep to be slaughtered."
>
> No, in all these things we are more than conquerors through him who loved us (verses 35-37).

Trouble. Hardship. Persecution. Famine. Nakedness, danger, and death—none of these things can remove us from the love of God. None of these things have more power over us than the power of the resurrected Christ. Paul went on to expand this list even more:

> I am convinced that neither death nor life, neither angels nor demons, neither the present nor the future, nor any powers, neither height nor depth, nor anything else in all creation, will be able to separate us from the love of God that is in Christ Jesus our Lord (verses 38-39).

So if nothing in creation can separate us from the love of God through Christ, why do we live as if our sin can? Why do we live as if our brokenness is too much for Him, as if it still controls us? Why do we speak in terms of defeat?

We the church have strayed one of two directions: unwillingness to give up our hurts, habits, and hang-ups for the victorious life or unwillingness to believe what Scripture says about who we are in Jesus. Instead of embracing victory and speaking it over our lives, we rehearse all the ways we are sinners. And apart from Christ, that's what we are. But in Christ? We are more than conquerors.

Some Christians object to the narrative of victory because they think it will make people immune to their own sin. Scripture is clear: Repentance of sin is a vital part of the Christian life (2 Corinthians 7:9). But repentance is an action begun by God's Spirit, resulting in Spirit-led change. Repentance does not entail rehearsing our unworthiness (to ourselves and others) over and over again for the purpose of glorifying God. We glorify God best when we turn from our sinful ways, embrace the worthiness He has given us in Christ, and live out that worthiness by the Holy Spirit's power. In 1 John, the author points out that Jesus's role as our intercessor is the foundation for living confidently in our imputed worth:

But if anybody does sin, we have an advocate with the Father—Jesus Christ, the Righteous One. He is the atoning sacrifice for our sins, and not only for ours but also for the sins of the whole world (2:1-2).

Jesus was the sacrifice for our sins; He died to redeem our brokenness and to make us whole. A little further in the passage John goes on to express how powerful this identity is, reminding his readers that we are forgiven in His name (verse 12) and that we have the privilege of knowing God (verse 13). But he ends with a powerful statement, repeated twice, that sums up who we are in Christ:

> I write to you, young men,
>   because you are strong,
> and the word of God lives in you,
>   and you have overcome the evil one (verse 14).

What I notice when I read this verse is the present nature of his wording: "You *are* strong." "You *have* overcome." Not you will be strong; not you will overcome. You already have.

John can say this because it's true: Christ defeated death and the Enemy (Hebrews 2:14) and secured us an eternal inheritance (Titus 3:7). Jesus lived out His John 16:33 promise: He overcame the world! And that promise wasn't just for eternity; it's for today.

BROKENNESS MADE WHOLE

When I finally shared about my broken sexual past, a weight was lifted from my heart. Shame no longer had a hold on me. Even though I knew my friends and family would read it and know more about me than I had ever planned to reveal, the sting of my exposure was nothing compared to the joy of being free. And it wasn't just that I was finally speaking about my past—I couldn't keep silent. Others had to know the freedom I'd found!

That first step was the scariest, and it opened doors to sharing more. I started telling my story to the teen girls who whispered their darkest battle to my ear. I shared it over coffee dates and in church membership meetings and at women's ministry events. What used to terrify me to even think about, let alone talk about, became my testimony. I wasn't afraid to tell people everything I ever did because I was a walking picture of Christ's redemption. My broken sexuality was made whole by Jesus. How could I stay quiet?

The Samaritan woman experienced a similar level of freedom when Jesus entered her story at the well. "Here is a man who told me everything I ever did!" She told everyone in the city, "Come—could this be the Messiah?" You can't share your story with this level of transparency if your identity is bound up in brokenness. Something, or Someone, has to break the bonds of shame. That someone—for me and for the Samaritan woman—was Jesus. Truly surrendering my brokenness to Him, even after I'd been a Christian for years, was the turning point in my story. When I stopped identifying as a victim of defeat and started embracing His overcoming power, I experienced the abundant, shame-free life He promised.

Now, this doesn't mean I have never struggled sexually again. I still remain vigilant over this area of my life. Since the day I chose to embrace my identity as an overcomer, I have failed in many ways—relationally, mentally, and sexually—but now I know how to face broken choices. I know that brokenness is not insurmountable. It's not who I am.

This is the hope we have in Jesus: When we sin, we can repent, turn back to Christ, and live as "more than a conquerors" once again. In fact, the very act of repentance is our first step to conquering sin. John wrote about this plainly: "If we claim to be without sin, we deceive ourselves and the truth is not in us. If we confess our sins, he is faithful and just and will forgive us our sins and purify us from all unrighteousness" (1 John 1:8-9). This confession of sin is the antidote to shame. Though we are eternally secure in Jesus, our sinful actions pull us away from our daily relationship with God. Confession and repentance restore peace to that relationship. This is not something we take advantage of by purposely sinning (as Paul talked about in Romans 6), but rather is a beautiful picture of God's love. As we grow in faith, we learn how to acknowledge our sins (a necessary part of repentance and sanctification) without identifying as sinners. We are conquerors in Jesus: conquerors of sin, shame, anxiety, fear, legalism, grief, and "every pretension that sets itself up against the knowledge of God" (2 Corinthians 10:5). We will still experience these things in this fallen world, but we will not be defined by them.

EMBRACE GRACE

Simply put, the overcoming life is lived by staying in step with God. This daily relationship is neither rigid legalism nor shallow apathy. It is a journey of listening for the Holy Spirit's conviction, acknowledging when we fail, turning from our failure, and embracing the grace God grants us. But here's the hard part: We know this in theory, but how do we believe it? How do we embrace grace?

Embracing God's grace over my sin wasn't a onetime thing. I didn't just repent one day, believe God for my freedom, and never struggle with guilt again. No, each day I must ask myself, "Do I believe what God says about who He is, who I am, and what I've done? Do I trust Him enough to cast myself on His mercy? Will I let faith silence condemnation?"

First John 3:19-20 says, "This is how we know that we belong to the truth and how we set our hearts at rest in his presence: If our hearts condemn us, we know that God is greater than our hearts, and he knows everything." *If our hearts condemn us…* God is greater. Remember, condemnation is *not* the same as conviction! Conviction draws us near God through repentance; condemnation pushes us *away* from God through guilt. Conviction restores; condemnation separates. When you are in Christ, you can speak God's greatness over any condemnation you feel. Your heart does not have the right to tell you who you are; God does.

I recently had to preach this truth to myself over a situation in which I felt condemned. I had spoken loudly about God's truth and, as one may expect, people were offended. I wasn't sure if what I felt was conviction or condemnation; I was deeply worried about offending people, but I also felt the action I took was right. Concerned that I may have overstepped, I sought godly counsel to see if I should apologize for what I'd said. My counselors told me the actions I took checked out against the proper order for how to confront such an issue that we find in Scripture. What a relief! Through that time of questioning, I learned to preach the truth of God over condemnation, rejecting anything that didn't line up with my identity, His identity, and the expectations He had for me.

Condemnation works in confusion and lies. Though our identities are rooted in what God does for us, not what we have done, condemnation tells us otherwise. Embracing grace is a conscious choice to believe the voice of God. And to believe the voice of God, we have to know who He is and what He says. We have to be in the Word.

We talked in depth about this in chapter 4, but it's worth revisiting. Without grounding ourselves in the Word of God we can't live by the truth of God. Without living by the truth of God we can't live out the freedom of God. An overcoming life is the product of consistent exposure to God through His Word. This isn't another reminder to do your devotions. This is war! Abundant life doesn't happen apart from God, and God has revealed Himself in Scripture. Our spiritual enemy will do anything he can to keep us away from the Bible because he knows how powerful it is. Are we going to let him win?

We are not born again to live in defeat. As Paul said in Galatians 5:13, "You, my brothers and sisters, were called to be free. But do not use your freedom to indulge the flesh." God sent Jesus to overcome sin, death, and everything affected by it. You will still face hard things. You will have to walk by the Spirit. You will even fall flat in sin—but you can repent and be restored. Victory is a lifestyle, not a destination. And in Christ, you are more than you could ever be on your own.

WHAT YOU CAN DO TODAY

1. Think about how you view yourself. Do you believe you are enough without Jesus? Or do you constantly rehearse your own sinfulness to yourself? Neither of these reflect God's thoughts toward us. Our worth comes from God's deep love for us and the righteousness He has given. This is the identity we should be rehearsing.

2. Accept God's grace. This is not going to be a one-day process, but I want you to keep this in the forefront of your mind. Until you fully embrace the grace of God and trust Him fully for this gift, you'll live in the spiritual shallows. You won't experience Him the way we see in Scripture. Let down your guard, trust His love, and believe Him when He says He covers you.

3. Stop using "broken" terminology to define yourself. In Christ, you are not broken. You are *whole*. Speak *life* over your days, your body, your relationships, and your work. Words matter. You have an identity that is whole and complete; that is who you are.

WHAT DIFFERENCE WOULD WE MAKE?

What would happen if "pink fluff" teaching ceased to exist? If Christian women not only knew who they were in Christ but also knew Christ's power in their lives? This would change the face of the modern church. Shallow Christian teaching keeps women from fulfilling their Great Commission purpose of Matthew 28:19-20. But when these same women seek out discipleship and theological understanding, their lives and relationships are transformed. They no longer have to try to make a difference; they *are* the difference in their communities.

I think back to the early days of my walk with Jesus, those days when temptation so easily overcame me instead of my overcoming temptation. Or the days when I lived under the heavy weights of insecurity and legalism. Or the seasons when my relationships struggled beneath my own desperate attempt to control. As Paul said so well in Philippians 3:12: "Not that I have already obtained all this, or have already arrived at my goal, but I press on to take hold

...or which Christ Jesus took hold of me." I still have to stay ...nt and Spirit-led in these areas of my life, and I still stumble ...n many ways. But my walk with the Lord is maturing me each day, and as I mature, I see my community changing too.

WE CHANGE COMMUNITY
BY CHANGING IN COMMUNITY

When asked, "What do you want your life to accomplish?" most people describe some kind of lasting impact they want to have, a life they hope will make a difference in the world. We think in terms of the big picture, but our lives are actually lived in the mundane moments, and our legacy is less about the world at large and more about our immediate communities. But here's the kicker: We can't impact our communities if we're constantly playing whack-a-mole with our sinfulness. And we can't overcome our sinfulness—or the difficulties of this world—apart from Jesus. To truly make a difference in the world, we have to know the Creator and Redeemer of the world on an intimate level. We have to be women of spiritual depth.

Spiritual depth is what changes our communities, and we don't help people grow by grabbing the nearest soapbox to preach in the street. We change our communities by letting Jesus change our lives in front of, alongside, and within our communities. As people witness our love for the Lord, our dedication to His Word, and our transformation into His likeness through the Spirit, they realize, *Wow! This gospel is actually good for what it says.* But to change in front of others requires vulnerability—one of the scariest practices known to man.

When I think about vulnerability, I think about...bowling. My biggest—and longest standing—argument with Josh isn't over finances or love languages or parenting. Josh and I argue over *bowling*. He loves it; I hate it. For most of our marriage I didn't know why I hated it so much. The shoes? The atmosphere? The greasy bar food? None of these are high on my list of to-dos for date night, but that's not what made me hate bowling. It dawned on me almost five years into my marriage: I hate bowling because it's *repeated public failure*. Think about it! In what other sport would you get up in front of your friends and hurl a ball over and over no matter how bad you are at the sport? In baseball, they'd tell you to get off the pitcher's mound. In football, they'd bench you. In bowling, failure is "part of the fun"—at least according to my husband.

But failure isn't fun to me. I prefer to do things publicly only if I'm good at them, especially in front of my friends. For me, bowling is just one long night of sport-themed humiliation. I am slowly learning to embrace the reality of *not* being good at something, letting it be about the people I'm with—not just about winning.

How often do we feel about Christian community the way I feel about bowling? We only play the parts we're good at, and only when they're visible. We don't want to fail publicly. We don't want to work at having a stronger spiritual life where everyone can see the messy in-between. I'm not talking about spiritual gifts; those will look unique to each person. I'm talking about spiritual growth in community—sharing the areas God is sanctifying in our hearts, asking for accountability, admitting when we are wrong, and repenting to God and others. Based on what we see in the lives of the apostles and early church, this is exactly what we're supposed to do. We change our communities, not by hiding away and preparing ourselves to emerge in religious perfection, but by changing *in, with, and in front of* our communities.

This is a hard pill to swallow. It's the antithesis of pride to allow others a front-row seat to our spiritual struggles. Doing this invites them to hold us accountable. But until we root ourselves in a community of fellow believers—people who don't just *say* they follow Jesus, but actually live as disciples of Christ—our own growth will be limited. And the more limited our growth, the more limited our impact.

Insecurity and fear of man will fight us every step of this journey, but as we discussed before, vulnerability is the death knell of shame. Exposing our struggles in community, sharing about our weaknesses, and asking godly sisters and brothers to support us with prayer and accountability is God's way of working sanctification in our lives. It's one of the primary ways He refines us into His image. As we allow ourselves to be changed beside our fellow believers, our community itself is changed. People feel safe to share their own struggles because they see us growing in our own. Deep conversations about faith and life become welcomed, or even normal.

I have watched this happen in my own community, Petoskey—a small tourist town in far-northern Michigan. In a place where, according to census records, more than 65 percent of the population is religiously unaffiliated, there is a thriving millennial Christian population impacting the community for Christ. It started with a few faithful Jesus-followers who opened their homes and hearts to one another. We study the Word together, share our hurts and fears, and motivate one another to share our faith. As our faith has deepened personally and has been cultivated relationally, it has blossomed into a community-wide testament to God's grace. People who have known only legalism visit church again for the first time. People struggling with addictions find freedom. Disciples are made and grown because faith is active in the daily lives of real believers. Petoskey has become a place of vibrant faith, overcoming power, and motivated evangelism. This is how faith in Christ changes the world.

THE GREAT COMMISSION
IS OUR COMMISSION

Saint Francis of Assisi is credited with saying, "Preach Christ, and if you must, use words." Not to disrespect an early church father, but this statement isn't complete. Jesus and the apostles all used their words to communicate the gospel, and their character proved the words to be true. Our lives should preach the gospel, but our mouths should do so as well.

If evangelism conjures up images of door-knocking and tracts printed on million-dollar bills, it's time to see this spiritual gift in a new light. Evangelism is our gift to the world: a testimony of what Jesus has done in our lives. But many young Christians do not make a practice of talking about their faith with others. According to a Barna research report, almost half of Christian millennials think sharing one's faith is *wrong*.[1] Certainly there are many factors for why people don't talk about Christ: fear, anxiety, lack of knowledge. But the most motivating reason to share one's faith is your own powerful experience with it. I wonder if more Christians experienced a vibrant walk with Jesus—one that transformed their daily lives—would talking about it come naturally?

The shallow, defeated Christianity we see today is not worth talking about. Who wants to talk about a faith that's perpetually lived in defeat? Why would you share something you barely believe yourself? That's not the kind of faith early Christians were sharing. Theirs was a Christian life touched by the powerful person of Jesus! Evangelism was like breathing. If you knew Jesus, you wanted to share about Him. But for many of us (me included) sharing about Jesus isn't that easy.

Just after getting married I worked for my alma mater, Liberty University, coordinating large campus events for the recruitment office. Every two months a bus would be chartered from Canada to bring students to our College for a Weekend events. I was in charge of chaperoning the shuttled students to and from the campus for the weekend, a job that included eight hours of sitting next to the bus driver with a clipboard and coffee mug. This bus driver was accustomed to driving for shopping trips, not Christian college events, and he was definitely not a believer. The first time we spent a Saturday together, he shared about his divorce, his kids, his bad back, and how he got into the bus business. I loved talking to him, but I spent some of that time worried about my "Christian responsibility." *Should I share about Jesus? This* is *the largest Christian university! How do I bring that up? What do I do?* I got so anxious and antsy about how to evangelize this poor man, I could barely talk like a normal person.

A few months later he came back, and once again I questioned what to say and how to say it. *God, should I tell him the gospel?* I prayed from my bouncing bus seat. But the words didn't come, so I didn't say anything.

My anxiety over sharing the gospel concerned me. Why was it so hard for me to talk about Jesus? Then one day in my reading I stumbled upon Jesus's words to His disciples in Matthew 10:19-20: "When they arrest you, do not worry about what to say or how to say it. At that time you will be given what to say, for it will not be you speaking, but the Spirit of your Father speaking through you." In context, Jesus was talking about persecution. But the Spirit is our *Helper,* which means He gives us the words to speak whenever and however we need them. Up to that point I'd been depending on my own wisdom and timing for evangelism, which only led to anxiety over how to share. I also thought I had to get a tangible result out of the conversation—as if sharing the gospel were a sales pitch! Matthew 10 was the freedom I needed. *This isn't all up to me,* I realized. *When He wants me to speak, He will give me the words.*

The bus driver returned for the first event in our spring semester, and once again I found myself riding along in our usual routine. As the day wore on, I kept asking the Lord, *Should I say something?* But the opportunity never presented itself. On the very last trip of the day, the driver glanced at me in his mirror. "You know how you live your life, you try to be a good person, and you hope for the best when you die?"

The Lord whispered to my heart, *This is your chance.*

As I began to respond to the driver's question, the words came without any effort on my part. I explained the gospel from Genesis to Revelation. When I got off the bus and checked off the two dozen students who had been riding with us, I realized they had heard the whole conversation. "That was the most amazing thing I've ever heard!" one boy exclaimed. "Yes, thank you for letting us witness that!" another said.

"Well, praise God." I laughed. "Because I don't even know what I was saying!"

This experience was my first taste of early church evangelism: sharing Jesus by the power of the Spirit and with the Word of God's testimony *because I loved Jesus that much.* The bus driver didn't make a salvation decision that day. It wasn't my job to get one. My only job was to listen to the Spirit, obey Him when He spoke, and share Jesus with a searching man. I thought I would see him at the next CFAW event, but Liberty canceled their Canadian shuttles and he never came back. When Jesus spoke to my spirit, saying, *This is your chance,* He meant it. It was my one chance to join Him in His call to that man's heart.

Christian evangelism in the early church wasn't a duty. It wasn't something people were forced into doing. It was the natural outflow of the Christian life. Evangelism was simple for the people who walked with Jesus. They knew Jesus had overcome the world, and they weren't going to stop until the world heard about it. Just like the Samaritan woman, Christians in the first century were telling everyone who would listen about the power of Jesus Christ.

In Matthew 28:19, Jesus left His final command: "Go and make disciples of all nations." No matter what nation you're in, you're called to make disciples right where you are. American Christian thought tells us that to do the work of God, we have to first "improve" our relationship with God. While we should be constantly maturing in faith, God doesn't tell us to work on ourselves before walking out His call. To the contrary, the early church was commissioned to start making disciples as they themselves were growing spiritually. Jesus also didn't specify that only pastors, teachers, and overseers were to be part of this disciple-making mission. His call is for every Christian! No matter who you are or where you are in your walk with God, you are expected to evangelize and disciple others.

REPLICATE YOURSELF

This book is meant to point you from a surface-level faith in Jesus to a deeper, stronger, more grounded Christian walk. I hope everyone who reads these words leaves with a desire to know Jesus for who He is, not just for what He can do for us. My greatest hope is that you will grow in faith and knowledge of the Word—and that you'll replicate yourself.

This is the point, really. It's not about getting to some spiritual plateau and sharing nice Christian platitudes on Instagram. It's about persevering in faith, letting Jesus overcome some of the hardest things in your life, then teaching others how to persevere like you are. We should be able to say like Paul, "Follow my example, as I follow the example of Christ" (1 Corinthians 11:1).

It's not arrogant to encourage others to look to our example. Our example is their most tangible picture of what life in the Spirit is supposed to look like. If you feel unqualified to do this, good; none of us are qualified to share the amazing truth about who Jesus is and what He's done. Fulfilling the Great Commission happens naturally as we grow in knowledge and love for the Lord. Our growth in godly community grounds us in truth, then we take this truth and share it with others. They, in turn, join our Christian community and make disciples of Jesus as well. This is how the early church multiplied so rapidly. People were on fire for Jesus and the abundant life they experienced through the Spirit. They couldn't help but share what He had done, and their community expanded. But it didn't just expand. It wasn't about mere quantity. Paul, Peter, and all the early church leaders sought to make *quality* disciples, people who persevered in faith and grew in knowledge of the Word.

For months before sharing the gospel with the bus driver, I'd been spending my mornings studying the Word, really digging into it for my own personal understanding. I may not have planned what to say, but everything I needed to say was already inside me. When it came time to share, the Lord used those truths and the Spirit declared them through me (John 16:13). Just think: What if all I'd been consuming for the last year was superficial theology? What if that man had poured out his soul's deepest questions, and all I'd been reading was a quick devotional? The best answer I could have given would be, "Jesus loves you." Or maybe, "God has a great plan for your life!" No context. No redemption story. No gospel.

God can reach anyone any way He chooses and He doesn't need us to accomplish His mission. But if Jesus's last words were to "go and make disciples," He expects us to obey. Everything we do comes back to those words. Our personal relationship with the Lord simply can't be an Instagram post or a continuation of the same quiet time pattern we've done for years. The Great Commission demands much of us. It demands that we do the hard work in our Bibles and on our knees so we know God powerfully and presently and can share His truth when the Spirit leads. Are we ready? Are we listening? Are we cultivating a deeper walk with Him?

INNER FAITH, OUTWARD ACTION

Shallow Christians do not replicate themselves. Their faith is inward at best, but not worth sharing with others, because it doesn't make much of a difference in how they think, act, and live. It's like I said earlier: People aren't motivated to share a defeatist faith. But for those who are ready to press into a deeper spiritual life, ready to seek God in His Word, ready to walk by the Spirit even when the Spirit leads them to speak into the lives of others, an outward-focused faith is characteristic. These believers love and share the gospel because they have experienced its overcoming power.

In John 8, Jesus's words to His first followers confirm what we have discussed through this entire book: that the Christian life is one of freedom and power, but we have a choice in how much freedom we experience.

> Jesus said to the Jews who had believed in him, "If you abide in my word, you are truly my disciples, and you will know the truth, and the truth will set you free" (verses 31-32 ESV).

As a Jewish rabbi, Jesus was expected to have disciples. Rabbis, like pastors today, would interpret God's Word for their followers. Jesus was unique in that rather than adding His interpretation to the Word, He brought the truths back to their original intent. When He told His disciples to "abide in my word," He was telling them to stay, rest, and live in the original truth of God. This is what true disciples of Jesus do.

Anyone can say they are a Christian, but Jesus actually gives us qualifications for being one. It is possible to be a fake disciple: someone who says they follow Jesus, takes His name, goes to church, and even posts quotes from the Bible on Facebook. But if this person does not abide in His Word and live by His Spirit, she will not be free. Worse yet, she will not fulfill God's Great Commission calling because she isn't actually following Him in the first place.

Jesus was so serious about this, He repeated Himself later in His ministry. In John 15, Jesus said again how *vital* dependence on the Spirit and Word is to walk out the Christian life:

> If you abide in me, and my words abide in you, ask whatever you wish, and it will be done for you. By this my Father is glorified, that you bear much fruit and *so prove to be my disciples* (verses 7-8 ESV, emphasis added).

Our inner life with Christ—our time in the Word, in prayer, and in the church—will motivate us to take action. Disciples of Jesus bear good spiritual fruit—the kinds of fruit Paul described in Galatians 5:

> But the fruit of the Spirit is love, joy, peace, patience, kindness, goodness, faithfulness, gentleness, self-control; against such things there is no law. And those who belong to Christ Jesus have crucified the flesh with its passions and desires (verses 22-24 ESV).

You know a funny thing about fruit? You can't force it to grow. It just happens when the tree is healthy. This is what Jesus was getting at in John 15: "Abide in me [the Vine]…that you bear much fruit." Do we want to be loving? Abide in Him. Do we want joy? Abide in Him. Do we want peace? Abide in Him.

The deeper we go with God, the more fruit we bear. The more fruit we bear, the more we preach Christ in our communities. And the more we preach Christ, the more fulfilled we are, because we're doing exactly what Jesus made us to do. This is the kind of Christian life worth sharing. This is abundance. This is living water for thirsty souls.

"AND MANY BELIEVED"

The Samaritan woman didn't know she'd meet her Messiah that day at the well. She came for regular water, but Jesus offered her something so much greater. She came from a place of brokenness, but Jesus offered a way to be whole. She had a choice; she could have left in the same shame. But she didn't. She believed Jesus for her story; she believed Him to be *greater* than her brokenness. Her understanding of God and her inner trust in Jesus drove her to share His hope with all who would listen: "Many of the Samaritans from that town believed in him because of the woman's testimony, 'He told me everything I ever did'" (John 4:39).

This brings us to a challenging question: *Would anyone believe Jesus as Savior simply because of how I speak, act, and live? Is Jesus through me that magnetic?*

Remember, this is not something we do on our own strength. We don't force people to follow Jesus through our good works. But when you're connected to the Vine, the fruit of your life will not just prove you a disciple; it will produce more disciples. At the end of the day, we fulfill the Great Commission by living every day, every hour, and every decision by God's Word and God's Spirit. Our testimonies point back to this. Our lives reflect this reality.

This book is titled *Stop Calling Me Beautiful* as a call to trade the surface-level message for one of true depth and therefore true freedom. But you know what's truly beautiful? Thousands of Christian women diving deep into the Word of God for themselves. Thousands of women learning to walk by the Spirit. Thousands of women replicating their own spiritual depth in their communities. "*How beautiful*," says Isaiah 52:7, "are the feet of those who bring good news, who proclaim peace, who bring good tidings, who proclaim salvation, who say to Zion, 'Your God reigns!'" (emphasis added).

How beautiful you are when you live out the thriving, growing, multiplying faith Jesus wants for you. How beautiful you are when you proclaim His peace, when you bring His good news, and when you share His salvation with those around you.

How beautiful the woman who tells her world through the way she lives, "My God reigns!"

WHAT YOU CAN DO TODAY

1. Ask yourself, "Would anyone believe Jesus is a Savior simply because of how I speak, act, and live?"

2. Begin asking the Lord to give you a heart for sharing Him with others. This doesn't mean you have to start talking tomorrow. Ask for the desire, the opportunity, and the words for that opportunity. He will give you all three.

3. Think about what areas discussed in this book may be holding you back from a deeper walk with the Lord. Where do you need to seek counsel, get prayer, and spend some time in the Word? Let that area be your starting point for going deeper.

NOTES

Chapter 1: Stop Calling Me Beautiful

1. Augustine, *The City of God*, trans. J.J. Smith (Peabody, MA: Hendrickson Publishers, Inc., 2009), 8.1.

Chapter 2: Hungry for More and Better

1. Augustine, *Confessions*, trans. Carolyn J.B. Hammond (Cambridge, MA: Harvard University Press, 2016).

Chapter 4: Why the Instagram Bible Won't Free You

1. Greg Johnson, *From Morning Watch to Quiet Time: The Historical and Theological Development of Private Prayer in Anglo-Protestant Devotionalism*, 1870–1950 (Saint Louis, MO: Saint Louis University, 2007).

2. Jonathan Edwards, *The Works of Jonathan Edwards*, Volume 1 (Carlisle, PA: Banner of Truth Trust, 1974), xiii.

3. John Wesley, "Preface to the Explanatory Notes Upon the Old Testament," *The Works of the Reverend John Wesley, A.M.*, Volume VII (New York: J. Emory and B. Waugh, 1831), 546–47.

Chapter 5: Skirt Length and Bible Translations: Overcoming Legalism

1. J.D. Douglas et al., *Zondervan Illustrated Bible Dictionary* (Grand Rapids, MI: Zondervan, 2011), 1117.

2. William Barclay, *The Gospel of John*, Volume 2 (Edinburgh: The Saint Andrew Press, 1964), 52.

Chapter 8: Used Goods: Redeeming a Broken Sexuality

1. Taylor Kubota, "How Many Women Watch Porn?," *Men's Journal*, November 24, 2015, https://www.mensjournal.com/health-fitness/how-many-women-watch-porn-20151124/.

Chapter 9: Known and Wanted: Cultivating a Lasting Community

1. C.S. Lewis, *The Four Loves* (New York: Harper Collins, 1960), 155–56.

Chapter 11: Everything I Ever Did: Overcoming Shame

1. Brené Brown, "Embrace the Uncool: Brené Brown on Overcoming Shame," *Heleo*, January 11, 2017, https://heleo.com/conversation-embrace-the-uncool-brene-brown-on-overcoming-shame/20526/.

Chapter 12: What Difference Would We Make?

1. "Almost Half of Practicing Christian Millennials Say Evangelism Is Wrong," Barna, February 5, 2019, https://www.barna.com/research/millennials-oppose-evangelism/.

About the Author

Phylicia Masonheimer is an author and speaker who teaches women how to discern what is true, discuss the deep stuff, and accomplish God's will for their lives. She particularly loves teaching on church history and theology, and you can find her spending summers around a patio fire with anyone who will join her. Phylicia holds a BS in religion from Liberty University, where she met her husband, Josh. After living in Virginia and Pennsylvania, they now live in northern Michigan with their two daughters, Adeline and Geneva.

To learn more about Harvest House books and
to read sample chapters, visit our website:

www.harvesthousepublishers.com

HARVEST HOUSE PUBLISHERS
EUGENE, OREGON